Transcendent Selfhood

Transcendent Selfhood

The Loss and Rediscovery of the Inner Life

Louis Dupré

A CROSSROAD BOOK

THE SEABURY PRESS · NEW YORK

To Henri Nouwen

The Seabury Press
815 Second Avenue
New York, N.Y. 10017

Printed in the United States of America

Library of Congress Cataloging in Publication Data

Dupré, Louis K   1925–
    Transcendent selfhood.
    "A Crossroad book."
    Includes bibliographical references.
    1. Man. 2. Self (Philosophy) 3. Transcendence
(Philosophy) I. Title.
BD450.D86   128'.1   76-18708
ISBN 0-8164-0306-6

Contents

The devise of the person
is not *sum* but *sursum*.

GABRIEL MARCEL

Preface

If men had forgotten what it means to exist religiously,
they had doubtless also forgotten what it means to exist as
human beings.

KIERKEGAARD

At the beginning of our philosophy stands Socrates' precept: Know thyself. It is difficult to imagine a more neglected principle in contemporary thought. This neglect stems certainly not from a low degree of introspectiveness. Seldom has man been more concerned with himself than today. But *which* self? Little self-understanding can be gathered from the closed circuit of everyday consciousness. Yet philosophy seldom breaks through that circuit and, for the most part, conceives of the self as a subject of worldly experiences. Rarely does it take account of those unconscious states or open-ended experiences in which everyday consciousness is left behind altogether. Yet an adequate concept of the self must include the self-surpassing states and experiences. For to be a self is by its very nature to be more than the actuality of one's being, more than what can be described in purely immanent terms.

I believe it was through the study of Marx that I first became aware of the inappropriateness of describing as mere actuality what is, above all, dynamic potential.[1] But Marx conceives of the transcendent aim of the self exclusively as human potential—as what man is *not yet*. Spiritual men of all ages have known self to be even more fundamentally determined by what surpasses it *altogether*, including its future achievements. Few speculative thinkers have taken note of this spiritual awareness in their reflections on the self *and* on the transcendent. The word "God" appears on every page of Western philosophy. Yet rarely do we find mentioned the inner presence out of which the idea of God grew and developed. Instead we encounter mostly descriptions of an ultimate reality, *opposed* to the self's being and *separated* from it in a "supernatural" realm of its own. While Buddhist and Vedantic writers from the beginning described the confrontation with transcendence as taking place *within* the self, Jews, Christians, and Moslems appear to have been more outward directed and less self-conscious in their approach.

Ours is said to be a man-oriented civilization. Yet our philosophers, theologians, and, recently, psychologists have been preoccupied mainly with man's situation vis-à-vis his environment: the universe, society, his family. With the exception of spiritual writers, Augustinian theologians, and some romantic philosophers, few have deemed his inner life worthy of their attention. Thus our concept of man has been developed almost entirely in mundane terms. The scientific revolution has put the final seal of necessity on this concept. The cultural crisis in which this naturalism has resulted will be discussed in the first chapter.

In the following chapters I have pursued themes and motives in which our tradition has become aware of the passive side of selfhood: its dependence and insufficiency. That side has not enjoyed great popularity in our culture. Far from considering the attitude of dependence a virtue to be cultivated, we mostly look upon it as a vice to be overcome. In America especially, "dependent" is often equated with "inefficient." The heroes we worship, the qualities we emulate, the achievements we honor, all emphasize courage, work, and active conquest. Even religious faith is defined more in terms of doing than of listening. Whatever mystical piety the early Puritans possessed was rapidly replaced by religious activism. Now active virtues are badly needed in a new land, and it would be foolish to deride what gave us our distinctive greatness. But in cultivating them one-sidedly we have merely diminished their impact. This should need little argument in the aftermath of the frightful waste of lives and energy caused by our insistence on interfering in situations beyond our control. But in a less recognized fashion it is also responsible for the flatness and superficiality of our culture. Though we produce most of the great scientists and many of the outstanding artists of our time, we basically remain a nation of "fixers." In reducing every crisis to a "problem," we continue to express our belief in our ability to conquer the world and ourselves by action and assault.

Older nations tend to dismiss this belief as too naively optimistic. But I wonder whether, underneath an unquestionable trust in our ability to change the world, we may not find a more deep-seated religious pessimism, a fundamental distrust of nature in ourselves and in others, which prevents us from letting ourselves ever be dependent. Perhaps we dare not be passive because, as the child that refuses to close its eyes, we feel surrounded by enemy forces. Certainly our national penchant toward self-criticism does not derive from naive optimism. Nor does our more primitive tendency to divide the world into the powers of good and the powers of evil. We shy away from situations that require passivity and dependence. As one wise man aptly put it:

> It is the secret fear of most people that they cannot have both dependence and independence, just as it is their secret hope that they can. Fortunately they not only can but must. But such a homely truth is not much preached in our land. We are forbidden to have precisely what nature demands most. We are often forced by our culture to deny dependence, passivity, the wish and ability to receive.[2]

In denying passivity and dependence we have excluded a deeper level of existence. The purpose of this study is to explore this level and to make it part of our overall view of man.

The course of my reflections mainly followed my own spiritual need. Having felt little concern for systematic unity or completeness as I developed them, I now can make no pretense of presenting a comprehensive theory of transcendent selfhood. Yet in a time of need even a fragmentary contribution toward a more complete vision of man might be welcome. My meditations were often directed by the symbols, practices, and doctrines in which the Judeo-Christian tradition has articulated man's relation to the transcendent. Yet that tradition itself must frequently be questioned and criticized, since it suffers from the defects of our culture and all too often it has patterned its own symbols on objectivist models. Nevertheless, man lives and thinks in a community, even when he explores and realizes the transcendence of his own selfhood, and the Judeo-Christian religious tradition *is* our way to transcendence. We may criticize it where we think it has failed (this in itself is a religious deed); we may abandon it when we are no longer able to identify with its vision and symbolic expression; but we cannot ignore what is already so much part of ourselves. Thus the reader may regard the following pages as a critical reflection on our religious tradition in the light of inner transcendence.

My present work continues what earlier publications initiated. Yet on one fundamental point I have to change my position. For reasons explained in chapter 2, I no longer consider the sacred a primary category of transcendence today. More even than in my earlier work I have become aware of the urgent need of our culture for a spiritual dimension, and of the essential part which religion must play in providing it.

Parts of this book have been published in various journals.* I thank the editors for their permission to reuse them in a more integrated context. Though my ideas were mostly conceived in solitude, they were inspired by the inner presence of spiritual men and women of past and present. In dedicating this volume to one of them, I thank them all.

* *Thought, Harvard Theological Review, Journal of the American Academy of Religion, International Philosophical Quarterly, Christian Century, The Review of Metaphysics, Listening.*

1

The Loss of the Self

It is consciousness of the loss of everything of significance in the certainty of the self, and of the loss even of this knowledge or certainty of self—the loss of substance as well as of self; it is the bitter pain which finds expression in the cruel words, 'God is dead'.

HEGEL

In the following pages I shall attempt to show that *the* crisis of our culture is a spiritual one, caused by a gradual erosion of genuine transcendence. My argument does not attribute the responsibility for our cultural alienation to unbelief and religious apostasy. Nor does it propose a revival of religious beliefs and institutions as a remedy. For those beliefs and institutions are afflicted with the same disease that ails our entire culture. To call the crisis spiritual is not to explain it. What made a basically religious society change its outlook so drastically? What specifically brought on a climate in which transcendence can no longer be attained? It is, I submit, the same factor which has led our culture to its proudest achievements. Edmund Husserl, who devoted a lifetime to the pursuit of a "rigorously scientific philosophy," reached in his last years the surprising conclusion that the objectivist, naturalist attitude was the original sin for which the West was being driven into cultural exile.[1] The most fateful effect of this objec-

1

tivism and the immediate cause of the crisis is the absence of transcendence. I shall therefore first discuss how the two concepts are related.

A few years ago the debate on secularism entered upon a new stage when continuity between the modern age and the preceding religious epoch was challenged. According to Hans Blumenberg, the very concept of "secularism" reveals an unjustifiable attempt to define the latter in terms of the earlier.[2] The thesis polarized the discussants into those who accepted a continued existence of the old concepts in the new ones—albeit in a hidden, negative, or degenerate form—and those who attributed an original spiritual content to the modern era. Variations subdivided each camp. While to Guardini secularism had meant a general decline of the religious impulse without any positive factors to compensate for it, to Löwith it meant that religious concepts went underground and replaced the theological ideas of the old age with the pseudotheology of the new one. Some theologians such as Altizer and Gogarten accepted a far more positive continuity and restated Hegel's thesis that the secular culture is the natural heir to the Christian doctrine of the redemption of the world. More restricted applications were developed by Carl Schmitt who regarded the political ideologies of the modern era as directly derived from theological concepts, and by Hans Sedlmayr who found the key to the understanding of modern art in medieval theology.[3] To the advocates of discontinuity the modern age marks a new assertion of man which presents an alternative to the earlier world views rather than a reaction to it.

As the discussion progressed, qualifications emerged. The concept of horizon provided a basis for tentative agreement. Löwith, the main target of Blumenberg's attack, in the end conceded that continuity had to be conceived in terms of a horizon of problems (a notion used by Blumenberg himself) rather than of direct causal influence. Now, a horizon of problems is an altogether more manageable subject. Whether the leading ideas of our age are "Christian" or not must remain a sterile discussion, until one establishes what is *originally* Christian and at what point it ceases to be *intrinsically* Christian. The horizon of the Christian culture undoubtedly contained pre-Christian elements even though they were intrinsically incompatible with the message of the Gospel. Primary among them is the one to which I referred as "objectivism." The name is not entirely appropriate, since it consists more in an improper view of subjectivity than in an absence thereof. Even Romantic subjectivism goes back to the same source.

Rather than a continuity, then, between secular and religious ideas I pose the existence of a legacy of ideals and objectives which preceded either era and was, in different ways, strengthened by both.

The Slide into Objectivism

When in the sixth century B.C. some Greeks on the southwest coast of Asia directed their attention to the *physis,* the intrinsic nature, of things, they started a unique intellectual adventure which required a novel attitude toward their environment and which resulted in a new type of reflection. This beginning of the methodic thought, which we have come to take so much for granted, was the discovery of objectivity. It consisted in the marvelous capacity to be interested in the world *as it is in itself* rather than as it fleetingly impresses itself upon the perceiver's momentary condition. It enabled the Greeks to become observers not only of the world around them but even, as we shall see in the next chapter, of the world within. Yet despite some powerful attempts to look inwardly, on the whole their glance remained outward-directed. The subject, once they became aware of its role, seems to have meant little more than the window through which they saw the world.

There were currents in the opposite direction: the Orphic mysteries, Socrates' philosophy, the Stoa, the various types of Gnosis were inward-oriented. Yet they remained exclusive, reserved to a spiritual elite. In Christianity we witness the West's first attempt to render inwardness the very heart of its culture. In time the Christian world view incorporated principles and attitudes incompatible with the unique position of the subject. (We shall discuss this matter more at length in the next chapter.) But an intense spiritual life continued to protect the concept of an irreducible subject against the encroachments of an ever imminent objectivism. However, at the end of the Middle Ages this spiritual energy came to rest in two separate streams, one taking its placid course toward ever more objectified religious structures, the other ebbing out in an isolated mystical subjectivism. Then, suddenly the quiet streams turned into mighty torrents.

From the stagnant waters of late medieval piety erupted the Reformation's forceful reassertion of Christian subjectivity. The objectivist trend of fifteenth-century thought was rapidly transmuted into the scientific objectivism of the modern age.[4] We shall say little about the former. For all its power it failed to stem the objectivist tide within the Christian community. Is it because the Reformation itself was still too much burdened by late medieval positivism (the juridicism of the theory of redemption in its early documents betrays as much objectivism, albeit of a different kind, as late Scholastic theology) to give a true content to the subject which it had so forcefully returned to the center of the Christian vision? If it is true, as is often claimed, that in Kant the Reformation reached its final consequences, then the emptiness of his subject raises questions about the content of the subjectivity that stood at the beginning of this development.

The other current marks the decisive triumph of the objectivist mind. Here we witness the release of a drive, present since the early days of Greek philosophy, to separate, take apart, and, subsequently, to reassemble into new controllable syntheses. Its prevailing disposition is one of critical doubt, its main tool analysis, its primary objective control. The immediate and very tangible results yielded by the new approach quite naturally fostered the idea that analytic objectivity was the only road to insight. To be scientific, knowledge was to conform to the physicomathematical model which yielded such remarkable results, and the sole criteria of mental activity became logical consistency and empirical verifiability. The goal of all cognition be- · came total objectivity, which would be followed in the practical order by total manageability. The problems inherent in this reductionist equation were lost in its overwhelming success. The sciences of man, the last to be developed (in psychology, sociology, and economy), held even greater promises. For they would give access to the untapped riches of that hidden source of energy, the mind. Ironically, as he progressed in executing his Promethean program, man continued to diminish in stature. Existence came to be reduced to a succession of objective functions.

· A major practical effect of the functional view of man was the uninhibited pursuit of power. Leveled to an objective plane, man could be manipulated as other objects are manipulated. To gain the same control over man as over nature had been an original goal of the "scientific" revolution. One of its pioneers, Francis Bacon, who, not coincidentally, had been a politician before becoming a scientist, epitomized the new attitude in his maxim: Knowledge is power. His countryman Thomas Hobbes explicitly related the pursuit of power to a mechanistic view of man. Of course, the mystique of power is not a new phenomenon. Plato knew all about it. But the naturalist view of man has made it into a dominating concern of our culture. Moreover, modern technology has provided the seeker of power with sufficient influence to become a menace to human dignity, and, indeed, to human existence.

The Hermeneutic Discovery

Philosophy did little to reverse this trend and, as we learn from the instances of Bacon and Hobbes, often reinforced it. Even Descartes's revolutionary philosophy of consciousness, which had marked a new beginning in understanding the subject, soon turned into a mere legitimation of objectivity. Spinoza brought it to its ultimate conclusion when, in his theory of substance, he objectified Being entirely.[5] Henceforth the physicomathematical model of understanding came to dominate all knowledge, and objectivity was set up as an unquestioned ideal of conscious life. It was left to spiritual writers such as Malebranche, Pascal, de Bérulle, and Maine de Biran to find a positive content for the subjectivity whose distinctness Descartes had so clearly established but so inadequately explored. Even Kant's theory of the transcendental subject failed to overcome the objectivist attitude. For although it was to play a primary role in the discovery of selfhood (which we shall discuss in the next chapter), Kant's subject never exceeded the status of a principle that constitutes objective intelligibility but remains itself unknowable. The insufficiency of the Kantian principle appears most clearly in the German Romantics who, dedicated to the primacy of the subject and uninhibited by Kant's critical restrictions, nevertheless did not succeed in finding a proper content for it.

The first clear philosophical awareness of the need for an entirely different concept of subjectivity, as far as I can establish, originated in the phenomenological-hermeneutic philosophy initiated by Husserl and Heidegger. Husserl's theory of intentionality could have remained a mere principle of constitution of objectivity, with respect to our problem not basically different from Kant's transcendental apperception or, for that matter, from the Scholastic theory from which it had been derived. Yet his controversial transcendental reduction gradually forced him into finding a content for this all-determining subjectivity. Without realizing it Husserl initiated a new theory of existence, when, in his *Lectures on Inner Time Consciousness*, he declared temporality to be the essential determination of the subject. Heidegger developed this discovery, to which he had been such a close witness, to its definitive expression. Existence is essentially to be in time and its temporality alone provides the transcendental horizon in which the meaning of Being can manifest itself.[6] Time had ceased to be a mere a priori form of cognition from which reflection could take its distance; instead it became the primary determination of Being itself. It is hard to exaggerate the significance of this theory for the understanding of our culture. Heidegger first fully recognized the need to attribute to the subject a content of its own. In doing so he overcame the basic principle of objectivism, that the subject is no more than the constitution of the object. But his philosophy also brings to a close the subjectivism which, in the wake of the critique of objectivity, had simply reversed the relation between knower and known without rethinking the content of the determining subject. Hermeneutic philosophy succeeded in attributing a creative role to the interpreter while at the same time maintaining that the interpreter is part of the interpreted. It thus fulfilled the condition indispensable to our culture for becoming aware of its objectivism.

But it also allowed us to understand another factor which had reinforced this objectivism and accelerated the loss of transcendence: the fundamental historicalness of human existence. The application of purely scientific methods to the study of Scripture, the increasing awareness of a kinship and intercausality between various religions, and the general impact of the theory of evolution abruptly confronted the modern mind with the historical nature of a relation which it had heretofore conceived beyond history. This confrontation was perhaps the most direct cause of the crisis of faith in transcendence, but one which would not have had such a destructive impact without the much older trend towards objectivism. Until the advent of historical criticism the Christian had seldom faced the consequences of his own thoroughly historical faith. Though regarding his life and that of the nations a pilgrimage through time, he had consistently secluded the content of revelation into a realm of unchangeable permanence. When that content was finally subjected to the same treatment as all other historical phenomena, believers reacted either by submitting to the judgment of history and lowering the status of their faith to the common plane of secular events, or by safeguarding that faith from the contingency of history in a closed cycle of divinely foreordained decrees. The former alternative jeopardized transcendence, the latter sacrificed history, including the historical character of faith itself.[7]

Philosophy provided no solution, since on the matter of history it was itself hopelessly divided between a relativist historicism and such secular versions of Christian providentialism as Hegel's theory of the Absolute Spirit. Lacking was a perspective in which history would retain its full contingency while yet being founded in ontological necessity. The possibility of absolute transcendence required a significance beyond that of a self-repeating rhythm of birth and decline. Yet history could remain truly historical only if it remained contingently open toward the future. Hermeneutic philosophy provided both conditions by founding history in the essential temporality of existence itself. More than a particular entity, existence is that in which Being itself becomes transparent. If that existence is by its very nature historical ("temporalizes itself" Heidegger would say), then history may yet reveal Being as transcendent. Hermeneutic philosophy accounts for both the contingency of being in time and its ontological necessity. Without such an understanding either time is the merely subjective condition through which the objective order is being perceived or it is itself the objective succession of that order. In both cases the historical consciousness reduces the existence in time to the objective and leads to, or accelerates, objectivism.

At present we find ourselves in the unique situation where the objectivist crisis (reinforced by historicism) has reached a climax, yet where for the first time we are in a philosophical position to grasp its true nature and are thereby able to reflect on means to cope with it. Yet the understanding which hermeneutic philosophy provides is not a golden key that opens the vaults of knowledge once and forever. For if its fundamental insight consists in the historicity of Being, then genuine understanding can originate only in a rereading of the past, *including the past of its own development*. A philosophical critique of our culture *must* include a reflection upon its own past critique. The idea of an instantaneous judgment on our culture fails through the very error which hermeneutic philosophy attempted to correct, namely, a consciousness from which the awareness of temporality is absent. Although much of this book will be devoted to such "rereading" of philosophy, we cannot complete even an introduction to a critique of our culture without introducing the great critics of the recent past, especially those who have been called the critics of our "ideologies,"

Marx, Freud, and Nietzsche.[8] They reflected upon the assumptions of our culture as a whole, its basic ideologies we might call them, and, at least in part, rejected them. That I use them here does not imply that they focused their critique on objectivism, as I do. Though in different modes and degrees all three were critical of objectivism, they also remained to some extent caught in what they themselves denounced. Especially Nietzsche contributed to Heidegger's critique. Yet, until Husserl and Heidegger, the proper perspective was missing for a critique of the very principle of objectivity as our tradition has interpreted it.

Naturalist Critics of a Naturalist Culture

The severest critic, yet at the same time the most typical representative, of objectivist naturalism was Karl Marx. Marx first fully understood that a particular way of knowing is rooted in a more general, socially and economically determined attitude toward reality. Thus our emphasis on "having" at the expense of "being" results from a dialectic between man and nature in which man has surrendered himself to thinghood. Marx is right. Yet in regarding dialectical opposition as man's only conceivable attitude toward nature and, even more, in defining that relation exclusively in social-economic terms, he unduly restricts his critique and, in fact, ties it to a more extreme form of objectivism. To interpret all spiritual achievements in terms of production relations, is to declare the *control* over one's objective world the essence of humanization. Today this principle has become so much part of the common view that we hardly realize the revolutionary novelty of Marx's ideal of man who *makes* himself while *making* his world. Though the humanism of the *homo faber* had long been prepared in our history, and may already have been implied in a number of writings, especially political, since the Renaissance, the contemplative ideal of Plato, Aristotle, and Augustine continued to prevail at least in theory until Marx. Strangely enough, his radicalization of the objectivist principle is due to a profound dissatisfaction with the applications of this principle in the past. What Marx attacks in the capitalist economy—the fetishism of commodities, the subordination of man to the production of things, the dehumanization of labor—must beyond its immediate social-economic causes be attributed to a more fundamental relation between the human subject and the world, which Marx continues to accept and, indeed, absolutizes.

One would seriously underestimate the import of Marx's critique by restricting it to the social-economic conditions of the capitalist system. Both in his early and his mature writings (especially in *German Ideology, Grundrisse,* and *Capital*) Marx insists that the current system itself is but the outcome of factors that long preceded it. Yet the fundamental question of how those factors were introduced into our culture remains unanswered.[9] I see no choice but to ascribe at least some to specific cultural attitudes adopted at the beginning. Marxists balk at any interpretation suspected of reducing social conditions to "psychological attitudes" and replacing the primary (the objective) by the secondary (the subjective). But the basic attitudes expressed in a culture are by no means a purely psychological matter. The problem of the *origin* of the structures emerges frequently in the early writings of Marx. It is usually circumvented by the tacit assumption that the most primitive conditions of production are essentially the same and *therefore* that in their origins all cultures are alike. This assumption stands in stark contrast to Marx's thoroughly historical view of culture. Of course, the principle that all relations derive from production relations allows of almost no cultural diversity at the beginning. But that principle begs the question. Marx himself often ignores it in his early writings by introducing normative considerations into his arguments (e.g., that a true humanism is based on *being* rather than on *having*).

To be sure, man must first provide his livelihood, and to do so he needs to put his mind to work. Also, the use of tools leads to production beyond one's immediate needs and this, in turn, generates new needs. From a social-economic point of view Marx's description of the beginnings of culture in *German Ideology* is basically sound. But the assumption that this is the *essential* point of view is gratuitous and more revealing of modern man's present inclinations than of the nature of the cultural process. For the mode in which even the earliest, most basic activities are performed is not determined by that activity itself. Choices take place from the beginning; they both form and reveal attitudes that reach beyond the purely economic. As culture progresses beyond its earliest state, those choices widen. Yet they do not forever remain open and Marx is right in restricting the possibilities of change. Once a culture is fully established, it will be increasingly hard for its members to find real alternatives. To perceive the real nature of the alienating restrictions of their culture takes a rare amount of reflection and imagination. Even critical minds tend to grant the premises, while hoping for different conclusions. Instead of questioning the basic assumption that man is essentially an objectifying being, Marx strength-ened it and universalized its scope. His critique of cultural alienation · teaches us more by what he unquestioningly accepts than by what he criticizes.

The preceding remarks are by no means intended to lay the blame for the objectivist trend in our culture on Marx. On the contrary, I have concentrated on Marx primarily because I regard him as one of the principal critics, if not of the basis at least of the consequences, of a one-sided orientation toward objectivity. If anything, my argument merely proves how deeply the objectivist current runs through our cul-ture. Even those who perceived the dangers in the present develop- · ment of our society were fully subject to its prejudices and, in their search for a solution, have merely succeeded in radicalizing the prob-lem. Yet the society in which we live seldom offers us the benefit of any critical reflection at all: it has mostly accepted the idea of a value-less, objective science and unlimited technological progress as a major goal of human existence. It refuses to face the crisis of our culture, by reducing it to a set of "problems," that is, technical difficulties that can and will be solved by more scientific research. This appears most clearly in the often conflicting ways in which we handle the various aspects of the urban crisis. Crime, crowding, addiction, and corruption are all "problems" for each one of which a political or technical spe-cialist construes his own, separate solution.[10]

The term "crisis" always has an historical connotation. After hav-ing been prepared, it runs its course and, hopefully, it will come to an end. Thus the "crisis" of our culture is usually said to begin with the modern epoch, though it was prepared by much earlier currents both in the Christian culture and in its Greek antecedents. Yet explanations of this nature remain superficial until we gain some insight into the *ul-timate* reasons why a culture can take such a turn and some acquaint-ance with the alternatives. A philosophical explanation requires· a · grasp of the fundamental significance of history itself and this, as we showed earlier, depends upon our understanding of existence itself as essentially temporal. An investigation of this sort belongs to meta-physics rather than to history. Yet metaphysicians have not been the only ones to reflect on the meta-historical principles of history. Before we turn to them we must consider the message of others who have reflected on man's fate in history. Perhaps no one has done so more penetratingly than the father of modern depth psychology.

In *Civilization and Its Discontents* Freud has written some memorable pages about the precarious situation created by the demands of any advanced culture. Our own civilization merely epitomizes what to some degree occurs in all but the most permissive and the least creative cultures. Reflecting on man's apparent inability to stave off major suffering due to living in society, Freud indicts the permanent rather than the transitory aspects of human nature. "A piece of unconquerable nature may lie behind—this time a piece of our own psychical constitution." [11] Any civilization worthy of that name must restrict man's sexual drive and curb his aggressiveness. Differences depend less on the qualitative distinctions of a culture than on its stage of progression. Every step forward means increasing complexity, higher moral demands, and, whether the demands are met or not, a heightened sense of guilt. In Freud's own resigned conclusion: "The price we pay for our advance in civilization is a loss in happiness through the heightening of the sense of guilt." [12]

In our day Freud's ideas have spread far beyond the closed circle of psychoanalysis. For many they contain the key to understanding the "alienation" which appears to weigh upon the contemporary mind. Even Marxists such as Fromm (*The Sane Society*) and Marcuse (*Eros and Civilization*) have picked up Freud's theme. Yet, faithful to the perspective of historical materialism, they have rehistoricized what to Freud was inherent in civilization *as such*. Important as their contributions may be in other respects, they fail to provide a proper foundation to the historical development. Why does cultured life encounter such problems? Because of a particular social-economic system? But why did men adopt a social-economic structure that must lead to a crisis? Neither Marx nor his Freudian followers provide any answers to those questions. They present the existing situation as the outcome of a necessary development, but fail to supply adequate reasons for its necessity. At least Freud attempts to found its existence in the law of human nature itself.

This is not to say that I consider Freud's interpretation of the crisis adequate. Far more than being psychological, our problem concerns the objective value system upon which our civilization is built. The fundamental question is not whether we are happy or not, but whether our civilization can survive with its distinctive value system. This question reaches beyond the subjective states of its members into the guiding principles of the culture itself.

Western Nihilism and the Death of God

The third major critic of our civilization, Friedrich Nietzsche, is of particular interest because he directy linked the crisis of our culture to its secularization. Yet at the time of his first work, *The Birth of Tragedy,* Nietzsche attributed the unsatisfactory state of our culture to the triumph of the Socratic ideal of science.

> Our whole modern world is entangled in the net of Alexandrian culture. It proposes as its ideal the theoretical man equipped with the greatest forces of knowledge, and laboring in the service of science, whose archetype and progenitor is Socrates. All our educational methods have originally this ideal in view: every other form of existence must struggle on wearisomely beside it, as something tolerated, but not intended.[13]

A culture based upon the spirit of science is a culture based upon the illusion that logical thought can attain "the nethermost depths of being." [14] Socrates who introduced this illusion was willing to die for it.

In his later work Nietzsche rejected much of what he had written in *The Birth of Tragedy.* He even conceived a new, equally important role for science after its liberation from Socratic optimism. Yet he never retracted his early conviction that the rise of the scientific spirit in the particular *Gestalt* which it had adopted in our tradition bore much of the responsibility for the present crisis. In a reflection of his later years in which he severely criticized his first work, he nevertheless attributed an even greater significance to this insight than at the time of its writing:

> What I then began to deal with was a thing terrible and dangerous, a problem with horns, not necessarily a bull, but in any case a *new* problem. Today I should say it was *the problem of science* itself—science glimpsed for the first time as problematic, as questionable.[15]

As far as I know, Nietzsche did not focus directly on the causal link between the unlimited expansion of the scientific spirit and the loss of transcendence. More and more we find him switching the blame for the waywardness of our culture from the "Socratic" spirit to Christianity, while science was presented as a redeeming power of the future. In this respect also, Nietzsche himself, like Marx and Freud, remains a child of the culture which he so penetratingly criticized.

Meanwhile, we shall concentrate on the theme for which he is most remembered today: the death of God.

In Luther's well-known phrase, God is dead, Nietzsche expresses his conviction that the process of secularization has reached its final stage. Its significance, as Heidegger warns us in a long essay, extends far beyond the fact that our contemporaries have mostly lost their living faith in the biblical God.[16] Christianity in Nietzsche refers to the entire social-cultural presence of the Church and its total permeation of Western man's existence, and God stands for the whole realm of ideals from which that existence derives its meaning. But if this is the case, more than a decline in biblical faith is needed to declare the Christian God dead. In fact, for centuries ideals such as reason, progress, and happiness have continued to provide substitutes for the Christian God. At this point that derivative spiritual realm is as much threatened as the biblical idea of God from which the ideals took their origin. None of the categories through which we ordinarily understand cultural events can convey the full significance of this one—not even those through which we evaluate the death of foreign gods and the demise of other cultures. For the idea of God lies at the very basis of our culture and its value system.

In *Thus Spake Zarathustra* Nietzsche describes the predicament of our age in his parable of the three metamorphoses of the mind.[17] First the camel goes burdened under a heavy weight, the weight of transcendence which wearies existence but at the same time ennobles it with respect. Then, in the desert, the camel is transformed into a lion: the slave throws off his burden and becomes free. But the freedom of refusal remains empty and merely trivializes life by undermining all moral and metaphysical values. Yet in the end the lion turns into a child, symbol of a new beginning in innocence. Only the childlike overman can redeem mankind by allowing the will to power finally to follow its unrestricted course. Now, the connection between the death of God and the will to power, which Nietzsche discusses in succession, is often overlooked. Yet the coming of the overman who embodies the will to power is possible only after the foundation of man's value system has collapsed and man has fully incorporated the previous spiritual realm of God. Nietzsche's optimistic vision of the future, then, is based upon a profoundly pessimistic evaluation of the present. The outcome of nihilism is the new, nonspiritual man of the future. Only the unrepressed force of life, the unbridled freedom of the will, can redeem us from the destruction of the present.

I shall not pursue this facet of Nietzsche's thought, because I consider it one more instance of the very attitude that led to the crisis: the · subordination of all forms of consciousness to the desire to control, to grasp, to dominate. Nietzsche's cure intensifies the disease. Yet questionable as his therapy may be, Nietzsche's diagnosis stands. A culture is, above all, a system of values. Pulling away its foundation may · bring down the system itself. Nietzsche first established a clear connection between the devaluation of values and the loss of transcendence. This alone makes him perhaps the most significant critic of our culture, deserving of his own words *Unser Weg ins Weglose.*[18]

Nevertheless, Nietzsche still remains within the basic perspective of Western thought. Equating Being with value he reduces the ground of reality to the sum of separate entities and thus excludes the very possibility of transcendence.[19] Heidegger has exposed this flaw in Nietzsche's thought:

> When Being is estimated as a value, then it is already reduced to a condition set by the will to power. . . . When the Being of what is is stamped as a value and thereby has its essence sealed, then is, within this metaphysics, any road to the experience of Being wiped out.[20]

The exclusion of transcendence, avowed in Nietzsche's overt atheism and implied in his philosophy of value, completes a process that started at the beginning of our culture. Nietzsche merely brought to the surface a current that had run most of its course underground. The crucial fact here is not the actual loss of faith in God, but the development of a mentality closed to genuine transcendence. Even in the heart of Christian culture we detect its early presence. Such expressions as "first cause" and, later, "supreme value" reveal how fundamentally the objectivist attitude and its subjectivist counterpart had affected our vision of transcendence. The loss of transcendence, then, more than a particular fact among others, is the event which symbolizes the direction of our entire culture. Zarathustra's expression—we have "murdered" God—correctly suggests that this atheism resulted from the inner dynamics of our own believing culture and not from extrinsic influence.

The Modern Age and the Loss of Inwardness

The preceding picture would remain incomplete if we failed to show how our culture at a specific point deliberately took a turn that led to its present predicament. The idea of a "natural" development alone does not justify the usage of the term *crisis*. Besides, the model of "natural history" is not appropriate for the interpretation of culture. Culture originates from a succession of decisions by which we create, refine, and constantly revise a system of values. Even when speaking of its "inner dynamics," we must not forget that the inherent factors which determine its development are themselves the outcome of prior decisions and remain subject to subsequent acceptance or rejection. Of course, I do not want to imply that a culture starts entirely anew at every moment. Its general tendency is to continue earlier trends. The longer they have existed, the more they become entrenched and the harder it is to change them. All this is common wisdom. But the continuity should not make us lose sight of the *reality* of conscious innovation. Thus choices made at the beginning of the modern age, though consistent with those of the preceding era, marked a genuinely new beginning. One particular potential came to be exploited at the expense of all others. Objectivity had been pursued since antiquity. But in the early Christian and Medieval ages it had largely been balanced by an intensive inward trend which appears in the nature of art, the language of prayer, and, generally, the entire rhythm of life. To refer to God as the *Being* of the self (Eckhart) or its *super-essence* (Ruusbroec) is to move in a spiritual universe essentially different from that of the first cause or the perfect being which determined the predominant theology. Despite the presence of objectivist tendencies, the general orientation of that earlier culture was not objectivist itself and remained open toward transcendence.

At the beginning of the modern era a decisive change of course took place. It is not merely that philosophy became increasingly object-oriented: to Descartes God is primarily the "author of nature," the indispensable initiator of the mechanic process. But in the modern age philosophy would express the general drift of the culture more accurately than ever before. Descartes, Hobbes, and Spinoza articulated the ideas which dominated their age. The trend reached its natural conclusion in the deism of the seventeenth century and the materialism of the eighteenth and nineteenth centuries.[21] Countercurrents continued to react. Pascal rejected the Cartesian idea of God, while the French and Spanish spiritual writers simply ignored it. But the hub of modern life was elsewhere. The unqualified ideal of an objective science was to place its stamp on the entire culture.

Even such intrinsically subjective experiences as despair, loneliness, and anxiety were integrated within an objective psychology conceived on the model of physical causality.

> Such meaning-giving interpretations with qualitatively rich contents (as, for instance, sin, despair, loneliness, Christian love) were replaced by formalized entities such as the feeling of anxiety, the perception of inner conflict, the experiencing of isolation, and the 'libido.' These latter sought to apply interpretive schemes derived from mechanics to the inner experience of man. The aim here was not so much to comprehend as precisely as possible the inner contentual richness of experiences as they coexist in the individual and together operate towards the achievement of a meaningful goal; the attempt was rather to exclude all distinctive elements in experience from the content in order that, wherever possible, the conception of psychic events should approximate the simple scheme of mechanics (position, motion, cause, effect).[22]

Now a homogeneously objective universe is by its very nature valueless: it functions but leaves no space for any transcendent support of values. Values continue to be created but become reduced to historically conditioned preferences. This historicist objectivism affects all realms of culture. Whitehead pointed out in *Science and the Modern World* how it affects our sense of beauty.[23] The work of art becomes more and more a private expression of the preferences of a particular culture, at most a transitory and therapeutic diversion in the "serious business" of controlling the world. Systems of thought (with the exception of science) likewise become isolated and, for all their universal ambition, basically private. They increasingly succeed one another without inner necessity. Today it is almost accepted that psychology and anthropology should provide a substitute for the intrinsic coherence which philosophy used to provide. We live in a fragmented universe without support and without soul that tolerates only ephemeral ideas and transient values. Thus the interesting replaces the lasting, the controversial the true, the assertive the meaningful.

What can be done? No way leads back to the past. A culture can only move forward, though "forward" must not mean in the same direction. It appears to me that the two qualities most urgently needed are clearheadedness and patience, particularly with respect to the loss of transcendence in our culture. Nothing would be gained by the blind, unquestioning "turn to God" which evangelists so peremptorily demand. First we must be able to *acknowledge* the loss of transcendence.

This is particularly painful to the believer who tends to hide his head in the sand of a past spiritual tradition in order to avoid the sight of his own atheism. Our predicament is due not to a lack of faith but to a lack of inwardness. To profess a belief in God and to observe certain rules of ritual and moral conduct is not sufficient to regain it. Faith itself is permeated by objectivism. What is needed is a conversion to an attitude in which existing is more than taking, acting more than making, meaning more than function—an attitude in which there is enough leisure for wonder and enough detachment for transcendence. Culture requires freedom, but freedom requires spiritual space to act, play, and dream in. Such a space is not provided by leisure alone: leisure itself becomes suffocating without spiritual content. The space for freedom is created by transcendence. What is needed most of all is an attitude in which transcendence *can be recognized again*. The question of actual faith is entirely secondary to the recovery of freedom by detachment from the purely objective.

2

The Transcendent and the Sacred

*Beneath the person lies, even in us, that 'wholly other',
whose profundities, impenetrable to any concept, can yet
be grasped in the numinous self-feeling by one who has experience of the deeper life.*

OTTO

Since the beginning of this century man's relation to the transcendent
has been formulated mainly in terms of an opposition between the
sacred and the profane. Introductory college courses in religious
science are often restricted to an exploration of this dialectic. Though
much in our past justifies referring to the object of the religious attitude as sacred, the equation cannot be assumed to be universal. Not
only does it fail to account for the primitive mentality, but, of more
immediate concern, it appears less and less appropriate to describe
modern man's awareness of transcendence. Yet contrary to a common
opinion today, it is not the *objective* nature of the sacred that makes it
unfit to symbolize an experience which the modern mind tends to
regard as purely interior. Even in its most intimate self-possession the
embodied mind requires objective symbols.

18

The Sacred as Particular Category of Transcendence

But the sacred is *one* symbolic complex in which man expresses his encounter with transcendence; it is not the only one. It no more covers the entire range of religious experience than the beautiful exhausts the realm of aesthetics. Indeed, some religious cultures seem to do very well without it. Remarkably enough, the category of the sacred appears to be most questionable in the one instance to which it has been most confidently applied, that of the primitive society. Advocates of the opposition sacred/profane as a universal principle belong to a variety of schools. Initiated by Robertson Smith,[1] it soon spread to French ethnologists, first Durkheim then Hubert and Mauss, and finally became the central principle of interpretation with the phenomenologists Otto, Van der Leeuw, Eliade. It may appear foolhardy to challenge a position established with such imposing credentials. Yet I remain unconvinced that the category of the sacred plays a crucial role in the primitive or in the contemporary mentality. To be sure, primitives, as all people, regard certain areas of experience more important than others. It is not unwarranted to attribute a religious significance to a distinction which may in some instances lead to the one between the sacred and the profane. But the two do not coincide, for the original distinctions take place within one diffusely "sacred" sphere. I see little use for a category that covers all aspects of primitive society and for which its members possess neither name nor concept. To say this · is not to make the absurd claim that nothing is sacred to the savage, but, on the contrary, to assert that, in varying degrees, all of life is and, consequently, that nothing is entirely profane.

An attentive reader will discover traces of this position in the self-same authors who popularized the distinction. Thus Durkheim, for whom the separation of the sacred and the profane constitutes the very essence of religion, nevertheless assigns to the taboos which are supposed to enact it not only the function of separating the sacred from the nonsacred but also that of introducing structure and hierarchy *within* the sacred realm.

> All these interdictions have one common characteristic; they come not from the fact that some things are sacred while others are not, but from the fact that there are inequalities and incompatibilities between sacred things.[2]

Recent studies confirm this intrasacral function of taboos.[3] Yet Durkheim never drew the conclusion from this fact. He continued to regard those taboos which distinguish the sacred from the nonsacred as "the religious interdicts par excellence" and devoted his attention exclusively to them. It is the very point on which later students of primitive religion have most challenged his theory.

E. Evans-Pritchard denies the existence of any rigid dichotomy in the primitive mind.

> Surely what he [Durkheim] calls 'sacred' and 'profane' are on the same level of experience, and, far from being cut off from one another, they are so closely intermingled as to be inseparable. They cannot, therefore, either for the individual or for social activities, be put in closed departments which negate each other, one of which is left on entering the other.[4]

Claude Lévi-Strauss, himself schooled in Durkheim's thought, all but eliminated the distinction as an illegitimate transposition of contemporary categories to the primitive mentality. Besides, it is hard to conceive what the notion of the sacred could contribute to an understanding of archaic myths such as the ones analyzed in his trilogy on structuralist interpretation. The significance of this critique for our subject is that the very theories from which the universality of the sacred/profane distinction was derived are being questioned today.

Yet the distinction has received its strongest support from the phenomenological school and, so one might argue, their descriptions stand, regardless of the historical origin of the descriptive concepts. Since the remainder of this chapter consists precisely in an attempt to prove that a description of the religious attitude in our time by means of the concept of the sacred is no longer adequate, we need not go into the matter at this point. I would nevertheless mention that those phenomenological descriptions which favor the primary importance of the sacred are based upon a *particular stage* of religion. Mircea Eliade, whose penetrating insights and seductive style have done so much to secure the sacred a primary place in the study of religion, supports its crucial significance by arguments that are convincing only when they are drawn from advanced religions.[5] Even among them I doubt whether we can justifiably attribute a *universal* significance to it. At least I have been unable to detect much "sacredness" in the original forms of Buddhism. One may read one's way through the canonical writings of the ancient Buddhists without ever encountering the term or needing the concept.

Of course, such difficulties may be circumvented by enlarging the meaning of the concept "sacred." A sacred that is no more than a common nomer for the object of all possible experiences of transcendence remains immune to attacks. But such a general definition fails to convey the specification required by the concept of "experience." The term "sacred," as most students of comparative religion use it, refers to a *direct, immediate experience,* characterized by some degree of passivity. Such a passive immediacy is not what determines the use of sacred in the biblical and Christian literature. Here the sacred is the main attribute of God, revealed by God as such. It is not, or not primarily, an object of direct experience. Holiness expresses what God is in himself. He may bestow this quality upon persons, places, or objects. But they do not possess it in their own right.[6] Repeatedly we read in the Bible that God is the source of all holiness: "It is I Yahweh who sanctify you." [7] Even where Israel is requested "to sanctify" God, the source of all holiness is God himself. "But I will hallow Israel so that they will sanctify me. For this reason does it say: And ye shall be holy unto me, for I the Lord am holy who made you holy." [8] The sacred, then, appears to be the quality of transcendence *par excellence* which more than any other distinguishes the divine as such.

Even attempts to retain the sacred as a universal and central religious category by sacrificing its ultimacy prove inadequate when we come to the Old Testament. Paul Mus was probably the first to feel the need for an ulterior category. In a remarkable essay on the Brahman sacrifice he posited the divine as such a category which founds the sacred and enables it to be mediated with the profane.[9] Henri Bouillard developed his conclusion into the general principle: as the emphasis on transcendence increases, the divine becomes more and more separate from the sacred. In some forms of mysticism one may eclipse the other altogether.[10] Yet this principle (which I believe to be valid in other instances) cannot be applied to the Bible which both strongly emphasizes divine transcendence *and attributes the sacred to God himself.* In the Old Testament the sacred fulfills a unique function which is by no means typical for all religion. For it is *neither beyond* God as a more primitive form of being in which both God and some creatures partake, *nor below* God as an intramundane category that is totally surpassed by divine transcendence. Rather it is the main attribute of the divine itself which belongs by nature exclusively to God.

I can think of no other reason why Western students of religion have generalized this category, except that it played such a central part in their own religious tradition. There lies a particular irony, then, in the fact that this concept, as it was eventually developed, least applies to the biblical faith from which it was drawn. Nonetheless, the dialectical opposition within which they conceived the relation between the sacred and the nonsacred still reflects the infinite distance between the Holy One and the mere creature. Only in a biblical perspective could the sacred be regarded as *the wholly other*. Yet opposition is definitely not the primary characteristic of the sacred in most religious cultures. The sacred is rather that which encompasses all human experiences and gives them their ultimate integration. One may well wonder whether a category that is defined primarily *by opposition* to the non-sacred adequately accounts for this function. "The sacred is not in the first place a separate, reified reality, nor is it *in itself* as the profane is, but it is an *objective relation, present to and coextensive with all being, all reality*." [11] All this raises some serious questions about the universal applicability of the concept. Does the concept after all the shifts of meaning still remain sufficiently coherent and specific to function as a primary religious category? I doubt it.

The Decline of the Sacred

My doubts increase when I consider the religious condition of our own age. To what extent is the contemporary awareness of transcendence a "sacred" experience? Of course, if one defines as sacred any experience which relates man to the transcendent, there is no problem. But the preceding analysis showed that such an equation must remain unsupported. Two factors, one doctrinal and one general-cultural, are essential for understanding the modern situation: an unprecedented emphasis on the transcendence of God and an equally unprecedented secularization of the world. Whether they are causally connected or not, the two have certainly converged in drastically decreasing the very possibility of a worldly experience of transcendence. Hence a decline of the sacred and of its primary effect: the integration of life. As man discovers the control over his universe to reside within himself, the need to relate each aspect of existence to a transcendent principle ceases to be felt urgently. Yet to relate them is a primary effect of those religious phenomena to which we refer as sacred. In the Judeo-Christian tradition the relation may well constitute the entire experience, since the sacred here is not perceived as a self-enclosed phenomenon but one that refers itself, and through itself all worldly reality, to God.

To be sure, any society as it grows more complex will eventually experience difficulty in integrating the various aspects of life. If I am not mistaken it is precisely out of this complexification that the need arises for a differentiation between the so-called sacred and profane areas of existence. Yet nowhere before have the latter ever grown *entirely independent* of the former. In our own secular age art, science, philosophy, and morality have virtually lost all need for religious support in their development. Nor do most educated men still relate them to a transcendent source.

- - But as the need for a transcendent integration disappears, the perception of the sacred becomes increasingly weaker. Today most of our Western contemporaries are totally unacquainted with the religious awe and irresistible attraction which are supposed to have manifested the sacred presence in the past. For people living in this technological age, nature no longer holds the sacred meaning which their ancestors detected in its works. Modern men frequently can claim no direct experience of the sacred at all, either in the world or in themselves. I saw this interpretation confirmed in a poll of my students in a course on the philosophy of religion, a group that, by selecting this subject, had already expressed serious interest in the topic. Asked what the sacred meant to him or her, one respondent stated forcefully but not atypically: "Nowhere in my world and at no time in my experience is there anything that I can point to as a manifestation of the sacred. I'm not even sure that the notion of the sacred can be meaningful to modern man. I doubt, at any rate, that I have a conception of it."

· Equally revealing is the fact that those who claim to experience certain aspects of life as sacred are unable to share this experience with their contemporaries. On a discussion devoted to this topic, in which I participated some months ago, no agreement of any kind could be attained about what specifically would be sacred. A prominent Catholic writer remarked that the Supreme Court decision to legalize abortion had suddenly brought home to him that human life at least was sacred, particularly that of a helpless fetus. A Protestant professor equally opposed to abortion, responded that he did not in the least experience life as sacred, but that he had made up his mind on this issue on the basis of a rational reflection about the dignity of man. His statement eloquently expresses the autonomy of the moral sphere even in the mind of the modern believer. Yet more immediately, it illustrates the totally private character of the sacred when it is still experienced today. Those who hold a particular value or reality sacred are reluctant to defend it on that basis, knowing full well how little understanding their argument is likely to encounter.

Now, increasing numbers of our contemporaries have grown disenchanted with the secularist fragmentation of modern life. They are searching for a new synthesis and nostalgically recall how a sense of the sacred provided their ancestors with what their existence so sadly misses. Not surprisingly, interest increases as experience declines. Quite a few theologians, anxious to assist man in his present predicament, proclaim that he has found already what he was looking for, and dignify with a halo of sacredness any state of mind that lifts a person beyond the unquestioning acceptance of existence. Today that is principally a feeling of dissatisfaction. As man becomes aware of the limitations of our society's commitment to the technical and the pragmatic, he is now told that his dissatisfaction itself constitutes a rediscovery of the sacred, since it questions the satisfactoriness of a purely immanent world-view. According to the teachings of Augustine, Luther, and Kierkegaard, is the feeling of being estranged in this world not in itself religious? [12]

Unfortunately, matters are considerably more complex. For even if we grant that modern man's spiritual need forcefully reopens the question of transcendence, it does not follow that the question itself places life in a transcendent perspective and, even less, that it constitutes a return of the sacred. The religious mind lives indeed in a constant awareness of its own insufficiency. But does that entitle every alienated consciousness to the attribute ''religious''? The question of man's homelessness has received multiple answers, most of them excluding the very possibility of an absolutely transcendent principle. But even to invoke such a principle by no means restores the direct, intramundane experience of transcendence to which alone the term ''sacred'' applies.

However, do we not positively witness a return of the sacred in the current interest in symbolism, mythology, and heterogeneous spiritual phenomena ranging from black magic to yoga exercises? Undeniably, something new is afoot and much of it seems to consist in a quest for the kind of integration which sacred signs provide. The sharing of common symbols and ritual gestures in small groups all suggest an attempt to recapture the ancient wholeness of life. But do those phenomena signal a revival of the sacred? Defenders of the "counter-culture" such as Roszak, Reich, and Winter do not hesitate to answer this question affirmatively. In doing so they merely follow the lead of some eminent sociologists of religion who record the reappearance of what religion has traditionally featured most prominently: integrating symbols. The all-integrating character of the sacred is an undisputed fact. But does it entail a full identity of religion and symbolic integration, as Robert Bellah implies? "Religion, as that symbolic form through which man comes to terms with the antinomies of his being, has not declined, indeed, cannot decline unless man's nature ceases to be problematic to him." [13] If this interpretation is correct, the so-called secularity of the present age means nothing more than that the established faiths which integrated an entire society and externally controlled the whole conduct of its members are disappearing, while new movements, perhaps less doctrinal and certainly less universal, but no less religious, are gradually taking their place.

Personally I believe the secularist revolution to have effected a more radical change, one that has not been reversed by recent trends. Because the so-called return to the sacred itself stems from a totally secular attitude. In the introduction to his *Feast of Fools,* Harvey Cox characteristically presented his new work on the renewal of religious celebration as a companion piece to his earlier, unqualified dithyramb on the "secular city." Indeed, one might interpret the religious trend as a more radical (and more sophisticated) effort to be secular by expanding the immanent world view so as to include even the *religious experience.* Thus modern man would attempt to embellish by a sacred glow his basically secular existence. Perhaps it is significant that the first prophet of the new awareness, Ernst Bloch, was an atheist who attempted to give the closed *Weltanschauung* of historical materialism a greater openness toward the future. After man has ceased to take seriously the traditional expressions of the transcendent, he nevertheless continues to feel the need for that other dimension which neither enlightenment nor scientism nor even the new social activism can provide. So he endeavors to regain the experience which now lies buried in deserted cathedrals and forgotten civilizations. But he intends to do so at no cost to his secular lifestyle, that is, without accepting a commitment to the transcendent as to *another* reality. Instead of risking the leap into the great unknown which his ancestors so adventurously took, he cultivates self-expanding feelings. He may even share his religious enthusiasm with a privileged few and articulate it in symbols borrowed from ancient traditions. But by and large he is not committed to their content, and his concern remains primarily with his own states of mind. I can think of no more appropriate term than "progressive secularization" for a phenomenon so very like Marcuse's "progressive alienation," which defeats the opposition by incorporating it within itself.

It is important to realize the precise import of the preceding critique. Much of what passes for a revival of the sacred in our age is only marginally religious, and the so-called sacred presence usually turns out to be no more than a romantic remembrance or an aesthetic imitation of past experiences. Yet despite this absence of a genuine sacred quality in modern life, many continue to possess a keen awareness of transcendence. To me this indicates that we must not tie transcendence indissolubly to the much more particular category of the sacred. At the same time the absence of any direct experience of the sacred cannot but cause a profound metamorphosis in our awareness of transcendence.

The Inward Turn

In tracing the source of all holiness to a transcendent God the Bible removes the sacred from direct experience to a transcendent realm. Henceforth the sacred would be approached more by trust than by direct experience. Christianity adopted the same priority. Faith consists primarily in obedience to the Word and in hope of things unseen. Neither intensity of feeling nor immediacy of perception equal the free acceptance of the revelation. Nevertheless, both Christians and Jews continued to be supported in their faith by the wealth of direct experience available in religious environments. Those have now largely disappeared. Whether and how a mature, educated American or European is religious depends almost exclusively on a personal decision. The choice is no longer made by others at the beginning of one's life. Nor can one's decision count on a supportive environment. To be sure, Christians continue to be baptized and Jews to be circumcised in infancy. But this symbolic incorporation in the religious community has greatly lost the binding power which it once exercised. Even the parents who subject their children to those rites often no longer regard them as certain and permanent commitments. To many they express no more than a vague intention on their part to introduce the child to a way of life which they have abandoned themselves. (A chaplain at a European university recently described infant baptism as "pouring water over a child in order to christen the parents.")

· A religious world view is no longer a stable, cultural complex transmitted to new members of a society by their elders. Nor does modern society support the exclusive claims of any single institution. Instead, the individual finds himself confronted with what has been called an assortment of religious representations from which the potential consumer may select themes of ultimate significance according to his private preference.[14] Religious institutions continue to be among the sources contributing to this assortment. But their very pluralism becomes, at root, a purely private affair often eclectically constructed and never objectively secured. What complicates the matter for traditional faiths is that their increasing "specialization," concomitant with the pluralism of modern life, constantly erodes their integrating powers. Global claims appear much less plausible as they are made by marginal communities issuing requirements which their members can fulfill on a part-time basis (such as attending church or accepting certain beliefs about the nature of God).[15] Thus, even for the traditional · believer, the power of institutional norms and representations has become seriously weakened.

· In all cases, then, the integrating synthesis of values—so essential to the religious attitude—appears to be left to the individual, who may or may not use for this purpose the religious institutions to which he or his ancestors traditionally belonged. A religious attitude today more than ever before requires the believer's personal decision, not only in general, but also for the acceptance of specific beliefs and norms. Once the believer has made this decision, a total integration of life in · all its aspects becomes possible again, even though in the present situation it is rooted foremost in a personal act rather than in surrounding cultural and social structures.

· · Religion has become what it never was before: a private affair. In a secularized society the religious person has nowhere to turn but inward. There, and for the most part there alone, must he seek support for his religious attitude. Whether such a state of affairs gives rise to a transcendence more consistent with the biblical principle that God alone is holy or merely marks the end of traditional religion is a controversy we need not enter into. But in any event it introduces a new way of being religious to which the term "sacred" in the sense of direct, worldly experience of transcendence has become wholly inappropriate.

Nevertheless, many continue to refer to the modern awareness of transcendence as sacred. Some earlier definitions may lend some support to this subjectivist reinterpretation of the sacred. Did Rudolf Otto not describe it as a subjective a priori? Otto himself could invoke Schleiermacher's theory of religion. Yet I consider the new approach to transcendence too far removed from the traditional concept of the sacred (however vaguely defined) to justify a continued usage of the term. Undoubtedly, there exists an inner experience consonant with the earlier meaning of a direct awareness of transcendence on the basis of a specific objective area. Whosoever "hears" in conscience the voice of God, as Newman did, may claim as direct an experience of the sacred as any holy space or time ever provided. But that is not, or is not primarily, the content of the inner awareness today. For the latter possesses none of the specificity so characteristic of the traditional notion of the sacred, including the sacred voice of conscience. Most often it is not even sufficiently specific to be confidently identified with an awareness of the God of Christian or Jewish revelation. Antoine Vergote who, to my surprise, persists in calling it "a sense of the sacred," describes it very aptly:

> After faith has lost its quasi-natural evidence, after objectification has taken the mystery out of the world, man finds himself more subjectively confronted with his singular desire for meaning and happiness. At this stage of a desacralized culture emerges the sense of the sacred. It consists in the memory of a divine presence the absence of which opens to the desire the subjective ways to a transcendent [*infini*]. Even if man has retained his faith in the living God, cultural desacralization obstructs his efforts to interiorize the revelation into his actual existence. With the God of faith man maintains no more than a broken bond. So he attempts to insert the words of revelation into that mediating experience which consists of the consciousness of the sacred as a quality of transcendence [*infini*] inherent in existence itself.[16]

My only disagreement with this discerning judgment is terminological. What to Vergote is "the prereligious sacred" of modern man is to me "desacralized religion" or, at least, "desacralized religiosity." The difference is important, insofar as my terminology reflects the very real break with the traditional experience of transcendence which makes the term sacred altogether inadequate. This, of course, is not to deny that to many contemporaries, even educated ones, the traditional sacred may still be present. In fact, I suspect that on rare occasions the transcendent still manifests itself in the world to most believers. But such hierophanies are definitely not typical of the religious mentality of our age. We seldom encounter the sacred in an objectively given, universally attainable reality, as the miraculous statue or the rustling of leaves in an oak forest were to our ancestors. Our way leads through private reflection and personal decision. Almost nothing appears directly sacred to us. In this respect we find ourselves at the opposite extreme of archaic man for whom at least in some sense everything is sacred. We no longer share a coherent, sacred universe with all other members of our society or our culture, as religions in the past did. Nor are particular times, places, or persons *experienced* as sacred, as they were until recently even in Christianity and Judaism. If anything is "sacred" to the modern believer, it is only because he *holds* it to be so by inner conviction and free decision, not because he passively *undergoes* its sacred impact. This mediated "sacred" substantially differs from the traditional meanings of the term: it is no longer a primary category of religion (as it was even in the Judeo-Christian tradition) and it lacks the essential trait of direct experience. What we are claiming, then, is not the disappearance of the category of the sacred altogether: we continue to give the name to persons and objects as we include them in our relation to ultimate transcendence. But since that transcendence itself is no longer *perceived as sacred,* the whole process of naming sacred, or holding sacred, is demoted from the primary level of experience to the secondary level of interpretation.

The center of human piety has moved inward where the self encounters its own transcendence. The modern believer sacralizes from within a world that no longer possesses a sacred voice of its own. His initial contact with transcendence occurs in an inner self that is neither sacred nor profane. While in the past nature, verbal revelation, and ecclesiastical institutions determined the inner experience, today it is mostly the inner experience which determines whether and to what extent outer symbols will be accepted. The religious person embraces only those doctrines which cast light upon his inner awareness, joins only those groups to which he feels moved from within, and performs only those acts which express his self-transcendence. For reasons I shall elaborate on in chapter 8, contemporary man feels a strong affinity with the mystics, not because he is more mystical than his ancestors, but because in the absence of outer resources of piety, he has no choice but to start from within, as did those who, however faithful to ritual and practice, favored the inner presence over the more worldly sacred. In this respect at least the modern believer is justified in considering the mystic a kindred spirit.

3

Beyond Self-Achievement

On the basis of the autonomy of the subject it is possible to achieve only an empty formal freedom. . . . It is clear that freedom with a concrete content has not yet been won.

PANNENBERG

Having described the gradual loss of transcendence in our culture, we are now ready for the other part of our task: the exploration of various avenues through which the self attains transcendence *from within*. Though a full philosophical analysis of selfhood falls beyond the scope of this study, I must at least briefly indicate how *self* differs from *individual* and is related to *person*. As individual man belongs to the world; as self he surpasses it. Once the individual is born, its only natural task is to reproduce itself in other individuals. Having accomplished this, it is ready to return into the anonymity of the species.[1] For the individual the most important day is the day of birth; for the self it is the day of death of the individual. Individuality passes through many phases of dying before it disintegrates altogether. But that final day is the most important one, the one that Rosenzweig calls "the secret birthday of the self."

While the individual thus renounces the last remnants of his individuality at this moment, and returns home, the self awakes to an ultimate individuality and solitude: there is no greater solitude than in the eyes of a dying man and no more defiant, proud isolation than that which appears on the frozen countenance of the deceased.[2]

Leaving temporarily aside the relation between selfhood and death, let us first consider the self as it is present in the living, striving person.

The Individual and the Self

The concept of person includes both selfhood and individuality. If taken objectively the person is no more than what Boethius described as an individual substance of rational nature. But person may also refer to a subjective mode of being to which the category of substance hardly applies at all. It is, of course, in the latter that we locate selfhood. Those distinctions may seem unnecessarily subtle, until we realize their deep practical impact. Thus a great deal of the present abortion controversy centers around the double meaning of person. Opponents of abortion insist that life is human from the moment of conception, since all physiological evidence indicates the distinct character of the new life from the beginning of its genetically determined course of development. However, as their adversaries point out, that argument falls short of proving that an abortion is of the same nature as killing a fully developed person. Human life is undoubtedly the condition of a personhood which takes its origins in it. But personhood is a dynamic category in which distinctions between undeveloped and developed stages are crucial. To call a living individual human is to distinguish it from nonhuman life. It allows no gradation. Life is either human or it is not. The same cannot be said of the person. Here we no longer have an objective *given,* but a subjective principle of self-development. In such a principle the various stages of development cannot be considered equal. A simple equation of individuality and personhood would allow us to predicate of the human individual, even in its prenatal stage, the essential attributes of the mature person. To reject such an absurdity is not to reduce personhood to its mature attributes. Life may lack those predicates without ceasing to be personal. To be a person means more than to function as a person. Function ultimately results from structure, and structure is operative long before functions appear. For that reason we cannot but conclude that personhood must be at least minimally present in every form of individual human life. But as a *dynamic* concept the personal introduces an element not contained in the human as such. This new element consists of both actual achievement and a *given* potential for achievement. The potential forms a single reality with the actual, but since in a dynamic subject it can only gradually be actualized, the degree of actualization enters into the very essence of personhood. Those remarks are obviously insufficient to resolve all the complex problems of abortion which, in any case, are not our present concern, but they point to the distinct character of what we loosely refer to as "the person."

Now, personhood is still too broad a category for understanding the *self* which is, so to speak, only its subjective core. For selfhood is self-awareness, and this requires a power of recollection which even a mature person may possess only in a limited degree. Often we find ourselves discussing man as if he were merely the objective top of the pyramid of living beings. Though justified in zoology and biology such an objective view conceals the most distinctive facet of man's being: his potential for selfhood. It took our culture centuries of reflection to uncover the subjective principle underneath the objective expression. Of course, spiritual men of all ages have known the difference. But they were not the ones who shaped the main course of Western thought.

Though man has always been aware of the distinct vantage point from which he looks at the world, originally he seems to have regarded himself as one more wonder in a world of wonders—so beautifully expressed by the chorus of Sophocles' *Antigone:* Wonders are many and none is more wonderful than man. To the Greeks man seems to have appeared as the crowning piece of a coherent, self-contained cosmos, intimately linked to the recurrent moments of its eternal rhythm. Socrates opened up an entirely new perspective when he invited his contemporaries to know themselves by looking inward, rather than outward. We know how strongly they reacted to his suggestion. Not without reason the Athenians considered it a challenge to their entire value system. In Socrates' view the good life was no longer determined by the approval of the community, but by the approval of the self, even if it meant forsaking the community or life itself. Yet the nature of Socrates' revolution must not be misunderstood. The Socratic self possessed none of the spiritual autonomy which philosophers after Kant were to attribute to the subject. It remained very much integrated with the objective world order.

The awareness of a distinct self did not become predominant until the Hellenistic and Roman empires when the bonds between individual and community were loosened. Only then did man begin to seek exclusively within himself a meaning of existence which social structures no longer provided. Christianity completed this process by declaring the soul the dwelling place of the Blessed Trinity. Thus transcendence came to occupy the very center of self-awareness. In taking this direction philosophically unsophisticated churchmen brought to a conclusion what centuries of philosophy had prepared. However, Christian thinkers rapidly returned to a more objective view in which man, once again, became the culminating point of nature, though this time dominating it from the even loftier position of a super-nature. It was above all against this objectification of transcendence, so much at variance with the original Christian vision, that the Reformers' protest was directed. However, it would be the philosophers of the new age, more than the theologians, who re-emancipated the self from the bonds of nature. Generally preferring to stay out of theological controversies, which would generate needless and sometimes dangerous animosities, they seldom questioned the accepted theory of an objective, supernatural order. Thus, except for some spiritual writings, the transcendent aspect of the rediscovered subjectivity remained unexplored.

Descartes first clearly stated that mind is a different kind of being, and proceeded to develop that insight into a full-fledged metaphysical theory. Defining the material world in purely rational categories, he reversed the prevalent view that the self must be determined in terms of nature. However Descartes never took the final step of considering consciousness as *constitutive* of reality. This step was taken by Kant. Despite some apprehension about his own conclusions (clearly though inconsistently articulated in the theory of the thing-in-itself), Kant declared the mind to be self-sufficient both in its knowledge of itself and of the world. Thus the subject changed from a principle *parallel to* the objective world into a principle *constitutive of* objectivity. Kant's Copernican revolution also reversed a basic principle of ethics: the morality of an act is not determined by its object but by the intention of the acting subject.

The Limits of Moral Endeavor

This brings us to the main issue. For it was above all the ethical consciousness which confronted philosophy with a transcendent dimension of the self. On Kant's terms the moral order did not allow any transcendent "interference." [3] The principle of autonomy, in the practical order, sealed the self off from a transcendence that had already been placed well beyond theoretical reach. Paradoxically, the same principle of autonomy would eventually prepare the possibility of a return of transcendence by detaching the subject from its finite, objective expressions. Philosophers coming in the wake of Kant would develop its implied subjectivity beyond the restrictive immanence of Kant's moral theory.

Thus Schleiermacher was able to find transcendence in the very heart of the Kantian subject by exploring another state of subjective awareness beside the moral one. The latter is active; the former, to which he refers as piety, mainly passive.

> While morality always shows itself as manipulating, as self-controlling, piety appears as a surrender, a submission to be moved by the Whole that stands over against man. Morality depends, therefore, entirely on the consciousness of freedom, within the sphere of which all that it produces falls. Piety, on the contrary, is not at all bound to this side of life. [4]

Schleiermacher identified this passive self-transcendence with *feeling*, the undifferentiated state of immediate consciousness which precedes all cognition and activity. Religion then came to mean "feeling of absolute dependence." This definition reflects a clear attempt to understand the self as intrinsically related to transcendence, an awareness "that the whole of our spontaneous activity comes from a source outside of us in just the same sense in which anything towards which we should have a feeling of absolute freedom must have proceeded entirely from ourselves." [5] The feeling of absolute dependence, then, reveals the transcendent ground of consciousness, the point in which consciousness is both itself and more than itself.

> This transcendent determination of self-consciousness is its religious aspect, or the *religious feeling,* and in it the transcendent ground or the supreme being is itself presented. It is present, then, insofar as in our self-consciousness is also posited the reality of all things as active and passive (as in our own case), that is, insofar as we identify ourselves with the reality of all things and they with us. It is present as condition of all being, which is woven into the opposition of receptivity and self-activity, i.e., as universal feeling of dependence. [6]

Schleiermacher's feeling of dependence is more than a *merely* subjective experience which would fall under all the objections of Kant's critique. It is a total consciousness which is both objective and subjective. Indeed, it is man's most profound awareness of his own nature. [7]

Schleiermacher opposed the active self-realization of moral freedom to the passive self-surpassing of religion. Kierkegaard went further and dialectically connected them with one another. From the very beginning the Danish thinker conceived of the self as a *choice,* but one which includes an *acceptance* of the circumstances within which I choose. Thus in *Either/Or* the refusal to choose is interpreted as a refusal to be oneself. Such a refusal, in basic conflict with the very nature of the self, inevitably results in despair.[8] The paradox of existence, then, is that the choice in which the self originates is itself possible only within a given situation.

This situation includes the failure of moral deficiency and of unachieved goals. The choice of an authentic self must take account of both in repentance and resignation. In repentance a person accepts himself as morally failing, while, at the same time, rejecting his failure as a self-betrayal. A repentant attitude asserts the self's dependence by admitting a situation which lies beyond choice and, again, by judging the choosing self according to norms which it has not chosen. The failure to achieve the goals which the person sets himself in the process of his self-realization introduces an equally crucial factor into the ethical situation. It is freely admitted in the attitude of resignation. Both repentance and resignation lead the self beyond the ethical order, for to acquire them it must adopt an attitude fundamentally different from that of active, moral striving. Instead of control it must cultivate obedience. Through it transcendence enters into the very immanence of self-realization, and ethical striving turns into religious abandon. By its own inner dialectic, then, the moral attitude leads beyond itself. Ethics without failure is no ethics at all, yet, in order to cope with failure, man is forced to leave the ethical order behind. Repentance and resignation, then, are at once the ultimate ethical expression and the final ethical contradiction. Or in Kierkegaard's paradoxical saying, ethics results in the suspension of the ethical. At that point the self abandons its own immanence and yields to transcendence.

Being a constant tension between the dynamics of immanence and of transcendence, the self is reducible neither to active endeavor alone nor to passive surrender. Possibility and necessity are equally essential facets of the self.

> Inasmuch as it is itself, it is the necessary, and inasmuch as it has to become itself, it is a possibility. Now if the possibility outruns necessity,

the self runs away from itself, so that it has no necessity whereto it is bound to return—then it is the despair of possibility.[9]

Freedom encounters transcendence in its possibility as well as in its necessity. For to believe in possibility when hope has lost all support requires as much faith in the transcendent as to accept a self over which one exercises no ultimate control.

Selfhood cannot be defined in ethical terms only. The self transcends its striving as well as its achievements. To confine it to the former, as existentialists tend to do, is to set up a contentless, aimless subject; to confine it to the latter, as Marxists do, is to miss the subject altogether and to reduce the self to a universal genus. The transcendence of selfhood over individuality which we established at the outset, makes any immanent, ethical definition of man inadequate. In Rosenzweig's words:

> Together with individuality, therefore, genus too sinks to the level of mere presupposition of the self—communities, nations, states, the whole moral world sinks to this level. All this is for the self only something which it possesses, not the very air of existence which it breathes. It does not, like personality [in its individual aspect], live in it. . . . For the self, the world of ethics is merely 'its' ethos, nothing more is left of it. The self does not live in a moral world: it has its ethos. The self is metaethical.[10]

Not surprisingly, the religious believer refuses to take ethical issues with ultimate seriousness. His attitude, shocking to the moral humanist, is rooted in the conviction that neither the moral quality of his behavior nor the objective success of his actions are decisive factors of existence. Maurice Merleau-Ponty once criticized Christians for letting other-worldly concerns interfere with their devotion to the social causes of our time. Leaving the factual truth of this judgment aside, I would be inclined to agree with its evaluation of the religious attitude, but, rather than criticizing it for simple-mindedness, I would ascribe it to a more complex view of personhood. A full awareness of the self and its transcendence postulates a different view of human existence. Believers attempt to express this view in symbols, beliefs, rituals, and, to be sure, also in efforts to lead "a good life." But they never consider those efforts decisive.

Religious Ideals and Moral Achievements

This is not to say that the discovery of transcendence signals the end of moral striving. Quite the opposite. One of the remarkable facts about religion's impact on morality is that it provides the most powerful motivation to ethical endeavor despite its ultimate relativization of ethical achievements. No other factor in history has more consistently inspired man to moral ideals and more effectively supported him in achieving them.

It is not only in the awareness of moral failure, then, but also in the need for a transcendent foundation of the moral law, that the ethical attitude may turn into a religious one. Kant defined religion as the ability to perceive the moral imperative as a divine command. The definition may be inadequate, but is far more than an inconsistent attempt to give an autonomous moral system a divine sanction. It directly follows from the categorical nature of the moral law. In his final notes, published in the *Opus Posthumum,* Kant himself concluded that the religious interpretation is not added to the perception of duties as duties, but is given immediately and necessarily with them. This means, as Kemp Smith has pointed out, that the categorical imperative by its very nature implies the existence of God.[11] "The categorical imperative of the command of duty is grounded in the idea of an *imperantis,* who is all-powerful and holds universal sway. This is the Idea of God." [12]

In his description of conscience Newman attempted to found this transcendent character of the moral obligation in the actual experience of conscience. Conscience for Newman is more than moral sense: it is an authoritative "dictate" which threatens and promises, rewards and chastises. Responsibility, fear, and shame, all remind us "that there is One to whom we are responsible, before whom we are ashamed, whose claims upon us we fear." [13] Now as Newman himself points out, this insight is open only to those who already possess a religious sense. Many moral heroes never perceived the voice of conscience as the voice of God. So this must not be taken as a *proof* for the existence of God, but rather as the religious mind's actual perception of transcendence in the moral order. The divine sanction adds new weight to the moral obligation by emphasizing its transcendent origin. Even where it contributes no additional content, it radically changes the quality of the obligation.

Thus in the process of realizing his freedom man inevitably confronts the limits of immanent self-possession. If he ventures beyond those limits, the norm of the good life ceases to be strictly human. His goal then becomes a good that is no longer his own as it was in the pursuit of happiness. In its possession the self is more possessed than possessing. Jacques Maritain expressed the difference succinctly in an essay on Christian morality:

> According to a precious saying of Cajetan, *'volo Deum mihi, non propter me'*, Christian hope makes me wish that God be *mine, but* it is not *for me* or by reason of myself, it is not for love of myself that I wish God to be mine; it is for God and for love of God, for I love God more than myself and more than my happiness. [14]

We started this chapter with a distinction between religious transcendence and moral self-transcending. We may now conclude it by noting how the former profoundly affects the latter. For in the religious mood man is never satisfied with the existing code of moral conduct. Beyond the required and the necessary, he constantly seeks out the gratuitous and the supererogatory. Instead of "observing the commandments," he attempts to symbolize his response to a transcendent calling in ever new ways. The virtues of the morally good life he presupposes. But his main efforts go into fostering love rather than into achieving justice, into sacrificing oneself rather than into satisfying oneself. The secular moralist cannot but be puzzled by this emphasis upon habits and qualities which cannot possibly improve the good life. To be sure, it is "good" to be good to others, but does ethics not defeat its very purpose when it leads a person to lay down his life for the unknown, devote his time and energy to the incurable, prefer a lifetime of hardship to an abortion? Yet such appears to be the content of transcendent ideals. Nor is the religious man allowed to let those rules be constricted by a gamble on happiness for higher stakes, such as eternal salvation or eternal damnation. The most properly religious precepts are not precepts at all: they are ideals or "counsels" in which the voluntary character is essential. Their "gratuitous" nature follows directly from the very call to transcendence which they symbolize. For if man surpasses himself altogether in observing those rules of divine perfection, he cannot be *bound* by them as by rules whose nonobservance would be destructive of his nature. Religious man knows that he can be a morally good and even a devout person without attempting to meet transcendent ideals: only the desire to let himself be taken beyond himself induces him to do what from an immanent ethical standpoint must remain superfluous, if not useless. Here the categorical imperative has ceased to sound its "Thou shalt," and man hears only the hypothetical imperative "If you want to be perfect . . ."

Paradoxically, it is precisely such "useless" morality which is primarily responsible for moral progress. Left to follow their own course, ethical systems remain largely restricted to rules for the survival of the group in which they originated. They are neither universal nor creative. In *The Two Sources of Morality and Religion* Bergson showed how some transcendent vision is needed to open up such "closed" systems. Understandably enough, members of the group seldom recognize this exclusiveness for what it is. In their own group they justify it as legitimate self-defense and in others they ascribe it to a "lack of moral principle." But the oppression of outsiders is inherent in the very essence of a closed morality. For the most effective methods for preserving the interests of the group are often the most ruthless with regard to others. There is no need to dismiss as hypocritical the moralizing of nations preparing a foray into foreign territory. Even the elevated theories of justice developed by the noblest minds in classical culture—morally not inferior to our own—did not succeed in decisively outruling such questionable ventures.

True moral pioneers have always had to break the established moral code in the name of a higher good. Not satisfied to preserve the well-being of their own group, they are willing to sacrifice the partial good to the universal good. Something in this attitude apparently strikes a chord in every human heart, for soon they find followers and gradually their rules of conduct become part of the accepted code of behavior. But ethical theorists tend to forget the origins of what they take to be self-evident, autonomous rules. Only a fortunate failure to recognize the uncommon source of commonly accepted rules leads utilitarian moralists to different conclusions than those of such crude but consistent prophets of moral egoism as Max Stirner or Ayn Rand. Today no one will stand up in public to justify slavery or brutal exploitation, and soon there will be few left to defend a society's right to execute its undesirables. But it is to a transcendent vision, not to innate moral inclinations, that we owe those changes.

Of course, to accept a demanding code of conduct in principle is one thing, to implement it in practice is another. The former is possible through the continuing impact of a transcendent vision no longer present to the agent. The latter requires an active inspiration in the present. The main reason why commonly accepted moral principles have become uncommonly ineffective in the daily conduct of our affairs is, I believe, due less to the inappropriateness of past formulations to new situations than to an almost unprecedented tendency to reduce morality to a purely immanent code of behavior. By some strange law man must attend to what surpasses both what he is or can ever hope to be in order to gain true humanity. In restricting his scope to what he is, he will not only fail to grow but, as the unhappy receiver of the one talent, lose what he possesses. The ultimate paradox of the good life is that it must be defined in terms of what is more than good.

4

The Diseased Self

> The majority of men live without being thoroughly con-
> scious that they are spiritual beings–and to this is refera-
> ble all the security, contentment with life, etc. which pre-
> cisely is despair. Those, on the other hand, who say that
> they are in despair are generally such as have a nature so
> much more profound that they must become conscious of
> themselves as spirit.
>
> KIERKEGAARD

The self displays a peculiar aptitude to lose itself, to become a stranger
to itself. In the first chapter I discussed the particular cultural conditions that may occasion this degenerative process or thwart the self's
development from the start. Here I shall concentrate exclusively on the
self's inherent proneness to alienation and on its ultimate significance.
In paying particular attention to mental diseases, I do not want to
imply that these commonly recognized states of self-estrangement are
the only ones. On the contrary, I believe that the mentally ill by their
acute awareness of the self's fundamental needs are often more in
touch with their real self than are many well-adjusted persons who
rarely become conscious of a deeper self.

As a self-constituted, dynamic synthesis, selfhood unites in a more
or less harmonious tension opposing forces. In yielding one-sidedly to

one of them the self disturbs the balance of which its very being consists. An even more serious threat to selfhood lies in forgetfulness. Routine work drudgingly performed, conventional values unquestioningly accepted, objective ideas never interiorized gradually erode the very possibility of growth and development. A person may spend a lifetime in this closed but safe universe without ever approximating genuine selfhood. If despair means lack of possibility, as Kierkegaard wrote, then the spiritually obtuse live in despair, though they may not know it. At the opposite extreme we find the self so overwhelmed by its own infinite potential that it becomes incapable of accepting its finite determinateness. It is the attitude which breeds what is commonly termed "mental illness," though the recognized illness is only one mode of being a diseased self.* The mentally ill also suffer from a lack of possibility, often consisting in a total inability to choose among multiple possibilities. While unreflective persons lack openness, the mentally ill are often unwilling to accept self-determination. In his moving *Images of Hope* William F. Lynch has shown how a sense of endlessness is the main source of hopelessness in the mentally ill. "Perhaps this experience of the terror of endlessness occurs in heightened form in men of achievement and in the ill." [1] The gifted and the sick (and the privilege of the former is often paid for by the curse of the latter) share a high sensitivity to the self's infinite potential, but also a greater difficulty in achieving concrete selfhood. This sensitivity may move some to high spiritual accomplishments, while others may be crushed by it, lapse into total insensitivity, or adopt an inauthentic, presumably less demanding self. Both groups perceive how limited decisions slowly seal an unchangeable fate. Like the Greeks who equated destiny with character, persons afraid of their own possibilities tragically realize to what extent personal disposition may hold the seeds of their own downfall.

Mental Illness and Self-Awareness

The condition of the mentally ill should be particularly instructive to those who are "healthy," reminding them of the precarious complexity of inner selfhood. Or, in Lynch's Platonic metaphor, the sick are ourselves, writ out in larger letters. Yet society appears to have little

---

* By the term mental illness I shall refer only to psychotic or neurotic personality disorders, not to idiocy, retardation and similar forms of mental deficiency.

use for this object lesson and prefers to seclude the mental patient as a nonperson with whom society's other members share no common destiny. Our way of treating the ill reveals our fear of entering into the murky depths of selfhood. To classify the mentally diseased merely as "cases" for psychopathology is a convenient way of escaping their message about the fragile condition of the mind *as such*. In the evaluation of selfhood the primary distinction is not the one that divides the sick from the well, but that which separates the developed from the undeveloped. The more complex the self, the more refined its awareness of itself, the more imminent the threat of mental disorder.

Existential psychiatry has revealed the universal significance of states of mind that we have all too lightly brushed aside as "sick." Thus R. D. Laing has shown how schizophrenia is inherent in the nature of a self that is both interior to self and exterior to others. In its essential duality the self is constantly torn between the mode in which it knows itself and the one in which others envision it. The schizoid person is uncommonly aware of this ontopathic condition. The inner self feels threatened by the outsider's look. To safeguard that self, one hides it and tries to conform entirely to the way one imagines the outer self appears to others. One avoids *being* in order to escape self-destruction. In *The Divided Self* R. D. Laing discloses the ontological significance of the schizoid attitude.

> Thus, to forego one's autonomy becomes the means of secretly safeguarding it; to play possum, to feign death, becomes a means of preserving one's aliveness. To turn oneself into a stone becomes a way of not being turned into a stone by someone else. . . . The individual's actions are not felt as expressions of his self. His actions . . . which I have proposed to call his false-self system, become dissociated and partly autonomous. The self is not felt to participate in the doings of the false self or selves, and all its or their actions are felt to be increasingly false and futile. The self, on the other hand, shut up with itself, regards itself as the "true" self and the persona as false.[2]

In severing appearance from reality the self creates an outward "persona" (in the original sense of "mask") which no longer reflects the inner self and which may eventually replace it. The cure of this illness, if there be any, cannot consist in a return to the "average" (which drove the self into hiding in the first place) but in the achievement of a new synthesis of selfhood. To the extent that they remain aware of their predicament, mental patients may be in a better position to gain authentic selfhood than "normal" persons, especially in a society that equates normality with hiding the inner self.

As a therapist Laing concentrates mostly on the social conditions that unquestionably define the concrete form of the conflict in our present culture. But his interpretation is clearly ontological; the whole process occurs as a battle between the powers of being and those of nonbeing. The alienated condition reveals a tension in the self *as such*, rather than in a particular state of society. We first need to understand the nature of selfhood if we are to determine which social and cultural factors obstruct its development. We then find that any society that denies the individual the possibility of spiritual growth and freedom estranges one from oneself, regardless of its material conditions and educational maturity.

Since sensitive persons are most likely to suffer from spiritual privation, a society's state of mental health is also an index of its spiritual well-being. In a memorable essay Georg Simmel has made this point with all desirable clarity:

> The ripening and the proving of man's spiritual powers may be accomplished through individual tasks and interests; yet somehow, beneath or above, there stands the demand that through all of these tasks and interests a transcendent promise should be fulfilled, that all individual expressions should appear only as a multitude of ways by which the spiritual life comes to itself. This demand expresses a metaphysical condition of our partial and emotional existence, however remote it may seem from our real life in the world. It symbolizes a unity which is not simply a formal bond that circumscribes the unfolding of individual powers in an always equal manner, but rather a process of unified development which all individuals go through together.[3]

Most social-economic theories of alienation one-sidedly ascribe the individual's state of mind to external conditions, while the positive or negative quality of those conditions depends upon the mind's own need to create a spiritual environment and must, in the final analysis, be judged by their success or failure to fulfill this need.

All faiths share a close interest in the various forms of self-alienation. They keep the believer constantly aware of the alarming facility with which the self may disturb or destroy its own fragile synthesis. Their interest is not fortuitous, for the salvation which religion promises presupposes an unsatisfactory state of being that must be remedied. Indeed, religion stands so badly in need of that preliminary feeling of alienation that one may well wonder whether it does not itself create the very condition which it wants to remedy. In any event, while most men and women feel only intermittently, if ever, estranged from themselves, faith thrives on feelings of alienation and takes as its first task to boost them where it finds such feelings insufficiently present. William E. Hocking perceptively observed:

> Religion is often described as the healing of an alienation which has opened between man and his world: this is true; but we may not forget that it is religion which has brought about that alienation. Religion is the healing of a breach which religion itself has made, and if we could reach the original sources we must find them in man's awareness of an Other than himself.[4]

Everywhere and at all times religion has taken healing to be one of its principal objectives. Though today no major faith would regard itself as a substitute for medicine, all of them continue to stress faith's medicinal quality and most have spawned healing sects. Thus Christian Science may be alone in emphasizing the healing quality of Christianity beyond all other aspects, but this quality is closer to the core of their faith than most Christians care to admit.

Faith and the Alienated Self

The confrontation with mental sickness has brought out the best and the worst in religion. To eschatological faiths such as Judaism and Christianity the triumph of good over evil is an ultimate ideal. Yet impatient for this ideal, faith may attempt to hasten its coming by witchhunting, heretic-burning, and religious persecution. Evil then is elevated to an obsessional object of negative worship, an antigod to be exorcised at any cost. To this mode of thinking nothing more clearly manifests the presence of the Evil One than mental sickness and emotional instability. Naturally inclined to regard mental illness as the work of strange spirits, humanity has been all too ready to interpret it as a symptom of satanic possession. The victims often willingly accepted the part forced upon them by their persecutors in order to secure for themselves a negative identity where society denied them a positive one.[5] The main quality characterizing the treatment of the insane in our culture is fear—the fear of a mysterious evil which is ultimately a fear for one's identity. By exorcising or imprisoning those who are different, people try to protect themselves against the threat to their own identity. But all that is salvaged by such an attitude is the shell that closes off the possibility of authentic selfhood.

Nor must we assume that our enlightened times have replaced the behavior of the "dark ages" with open-mindedness. In no previous epoch have the mentally sick been more carefully secluded from society. Where nonaggressive patients once remained in the family or moved into another normal community specially equipped for adopting a certain number of mentally ill, today we lock them up except when practical obstacles (mainly financial) discourage us from doing so. Despite outbursts of fanaticism, the Christian faith has throughout its history maintained a deep humanitarianism sorely missing in today's secular views. I cannot but recall my early experiences as a high school student in the Flemish town of Geel. A place of pilgrimage for those suffering nervous disorders and an open colony for the insane since the thirteenth century, the town has traditionally accommodated the patients in local families and allowed them to partake in almost all aspects of its daily life. Everywhere one encounters them working in the fields, doing errands, worshiping in church, attending children, or, if they are children themselves, playing or going to school. I cannot imagine a more humane attempt to alleviate an unparalleled variety of mental misery. The town's religious origins (preserved in the legend of a chaste Irish princess who was beheaded on this location by her demented father) are by no means fortuitous to the nature of the arrangement. For it is inspired by a vision of the sick as men and women who in their suffering were chosen to represent the universal alienation of all mankind. Mental degradation symbolizes the human condition in · its fundamental need of redemption.

This attitude, I believe, has its roots in the profound religious concept of human alienation. The existence of religious health resorts since antiquity, the expulsion of "evil spirits" in the Gospel, the continued sacramental prayer over the sick—these practices signify far more than a surpassed stage in the history of medicine. They symbolize that salvation itself is healing and that all actual healing is part of the redemptive process. This is particularly true for mental sickness. When confronted with the mentally ill, Jesus does not elicit faith before curing them, as he is wont to do for other diseases, but first "liberates" them. For the mental patient is a captive, closed up in an unreal self and, like the deaf-mutes of the Gospel, unable to listen as well as to speak. He is in despair if despair means, as Kierkegaard thought, shut-upness. Unable to relate, vertically and horizontally, he cannot reach out and be in touch with his own transcendence. He needs to be cured before anything else, and the primary religious assistance consists in healing, whether the healer be a minister, physician, or a counselor.

In regarding mental illness as symptomatic of the diseased general condition of humankind, faith relativizes the simplistically absolute distinction between the sick and the well, and calls attention to a deeper, less obvious level of selfhood. In the eyes of faith we are all diseased, and salvation must be to all what is so evidently needed by some—a healing of the self. Yet religious healing never simply coincides with an ordinary cure, even for those whose physical or mental health is fully restored. If the true disease lies beyond the obvious illness, the cure also must reach beyond the symptoms. Mental suffering itself then is assigned its unique place in the all-comprehensive place of salvation. It creates the solitude in which alone persons may find genuine transcendence. Only in suffering—and all suffering, whatever its origin, in the end is mental—am I most totally alone. My suffering is exclusively mine: it bears my name as no other experience does, because it isolates me from others. Only this painful isolation gives access to the bottom depth of selfhood—the locus of transcendence—which remains unsuspectedly hidden to the untroubled mind. This is the meaning of Kierkegaard's brutal saying that most people do not feel sick enough to accept faith. His own mental disarray, culminating in the breach of his engagement, illustrates the existential significance of suffering as presupposed by the religious doctrine of redemption. In a short entry of his diary Kierkegaard describes how he experienced the complex dialectic of suffering in his relation to Regine Olsen.

> My greatest pleasure would have been to marry the girl to whom I was engaged; God knows how much I wanted to: but here again is my wretchedness. And so I remained unmarried, and so I had the opportunity of thinking over what Christianity really meant by praising the unmarried state.[6]

Only suffering can convey the feeling of insufficiency without which the human person experiences no need of salvation. The condition of the mentally ill keeps alive the awareness both of the self's hidden depth and of its insufficiency. It is an object lesson that aids us in finding meaning for our most private and most painful experiences. The present trend is to ignore that lesson and to remove its inconvenient reminders as far as possible from the daily traffic of life.

In the same spirit modern thinking tends to regard a person's religion as the sum total of his or her mental inadequacies. This view may contain more truth than its contemptuous holders suspect. For without an awareness of basic inadequacy no genuine awareness of transcendence can exist. Yet it loses sight of the fact that religion is not a desperate attempt to cope with matters that cannot be handled otherwise, but a positive vision in which personal suffering is *needed* for spiritual growth.

Here it appears clearly how the alienation of which faith speaks so often (in its doctrines of sinfulness, of the fall, of redemption) is more than a mere *interpretation* of experiences that allow a different one. Alienation is first and foremost the awareness of a *fact* without which religion and its interpretations could not exist. Far from inventing or coloring a particular experience, religion gives expression to a primary experience. It still may well be the most comprehensive expression, because faith alone has sounded the full depth of the experience. Though we are all acquainted with suffering and feelings of self-estrangement, our ordinary objective ways of articulating them make it easier to suppress than to express the experience. We talk in order to classify in a universal, objective scheme, as a controllable "problem," that which is neither universal nor controllable. Suffering remains strictly each person's own experience which he or she is unable to share with others. Putting a common label on mental anguish is necessary for medical treatment, but is misleading if we expect the label to reveal the true "nature" of the experience. For suffering possesses none but a private nature, which means no "nature" at all. It speaks out of the most intimate privacy of my selfhood.

To be sure, religious terms are abused as commonly as medical ones. Phrases such as "sinfulness," "insufficiency," or "the need of salvation" may be just as impersonal as psychological ones, and a good deal vaguer. It cannot be our intention here to pit one against the other, but rather to draw attention to the fundamental *experience* expressed, however imperfectly, in religious doctrines. What those doctrines *mean* is more than a universal description of the actual state of the world: they describe the most private and most fundamental awareness of insufficiency. As such they reach to the heart of the self.

5

Images of Transcendence

*Art is and remains for us, on the side of its highest destiny,
a thing of the past.*

HEGEL

When the awareness of transcendence recedes and the perception of
the sacred disappears, the indirect signs of a holy presence take on a
new importance. In the two preceding chapters we discussed those
negative experiences which, though by no means religious in themselves, nevertheless impose upon men and women of our time a sense
of their own contingency and thus forcefully confront them with questions of ultimacy. Yet not all such ambiguous experiences are negative. The aesthetic expression has always played a significant role in
the awareness of religious transcendence. So naturally the question
arises to what extent it continues to play that role in our own secular
culture. I already pointed out that the artistic, as most other activities,
has emancipated itself from religious sovereignty. The point is perti-
nent enough to our present discussion, but by no means does it decide
the entire question. For now we are also concerned with indirect forms
of symbolization. Nothing per se prevents art from opening up transcendent horizons long after it has ceased to speak the language of the
gods. Indeed, this is precisely the situation in which, according to
Heidegger, the artist becomes the last witness. No philosopher has

been more painfully aware of the loss of transcendence in our culture than Heidegger. To him ''the default of God'' means not only that the gods and the god have fled, but that in this destitute time we are no longer able to discern the default as a default. Henceforth the poet alone ''attends to the trace of the fugitive gods.'' [1] When ''holy names'' are lacking, the poet alone still sings of the holy without words. Now to Heidegger the poet is not just the literary artist; the latter provides only the mouthpiece and ultimate articulation for art as a whole. ''All art . . . is, as such, *essentially poetry.*'' [2] To explain those deep but obscure words requires some preliminary insight into the traditional relationship between art and the sacred.

For the longest part of man's development what we now restrictively call ''art'' provided *the* symbolization of what we, equally anachronistically, refer to as ''religion.'' One cannot be discussed without the other: art was religious art. A heightened sense of transcendence and an increasing secularization separated the two to a point where art could be without being sacred and where religion developed some of its symbols outside the range of aesthetics. Yet the ties remained close as long as the religious community continued to pray in song, to move in liturgical dance, and to act in sacred drama. The artist also remained faithful to an allegiance which granted him inspiration and, often, a livelihood. The direct link between art and faith was dissolved only in our own secular culture. How then would art in our age still be able to evoke a transcendence which no longer belongs to its own essence? Of course, works of art continue to be commissioned by churches and we still refer to them as ''sacred art.'' But is a genuine sense of the transcendent conveyed through its aesthetic quality? Or, in spite of it, by its occasional association with the cult? To answer those questions we shall first have to consider what made or, to the extent that it still does, makes particular forms of art *explicitly* religious, and next whether art can, without possessing that quality, be *implicitly* religious and remain so even in a wholly secular culture.

Sacred Art and the Sacred Quality of Art

In the presence of great art, as in the religious experience, man confronts what appears to him as ultimately *real*. It is a reality in which he can partake only by moving beyond the oppositional modes of consciousness, objective knowledge, and subjective desire. Just as the religious experience results in a heightened awareness of what truly is and a willingness to let it be, the aesthetic experience leads to a new ontological perceptiveness. F. David Martin, who devoted a thoughtful study to the subject, describes the similarity as follows:

> Both are intimate and ultimate; both are attuned to the call of Being; both are reverential in attitude to things; . . . both give enduring value and serenity to existence; and thus both are profoundly regenerative. The participative experience, then, always has a religious quality, for the participative experience penetrates the religious dimension.[3]

If they would totally coincide, as they undoubtedly did for archaic man, their relation would create no problem, and we could rest satisfied with Goethe's maxim: "Wer Wissenschaft und Kunst besitzt, hat auch Religion." Yet clearly the two are no longer identical and they have been distinct, if not separate, for centuries. Are they distinct, as Collingwood proclaims, in that art asserts nothing? Undoubtedly, much as the artist strives for veracity of perception, in one sense at least, the *real as such* is of no concern to him. It matters little whether Mont Sainte-Victoire really *is* as Cézanne painted it (Is that even a meaningful question?) or whether someone exactly like Coleridge's "Ancient Mariner" ever lived. Even in portraits, expressiveness aesthetically prevails over physical resemblance. The only reality the artist and the art lover are concerned with is the reality of the appearance—which is not the real as such.[4] One might therefore be tempted to consider the aesthetic attitude as noncommittal with respect to the real. Yet to do so without basic qualifications would be to abandon the ontological meaning of art altogether and to posit absolutely what must be regarded as the aestheticist heresy of our age.[5] Great art was always ontologically meaningful.

Nevertheless, ever since art ceased to coincide with religion, and well before *l'art pour l'art* became its leading principle, its own ontological vision had ceased to be adequate for the expression of Being as transcendent. To be sure, the aesthetic consciousness possesses a transcendence of its own. It sets up ideals that allow man to surpass the givenness of the present. It opens up a realm of possibility in which freedom finds its vital space. Yet this transcendence remains purely ideal. Ernst Bloch, the rhapsode of this aesthetic Utopia, refers to it as a *Vor-schein,* a foreglow or foreshow.

> For all its transcending the foreglow, contrary to the religious, remains immanent: it expands, as Schiller defined aesthetic realism on the ex-

ample of Goethe, it expands nature without going beyond it. Beauty, nobility present an existence of realities to come, a world totally formed without extrinsic accident, without the unessential, without incompleteness. Thus the message of the aesthetically attempted foreglow sounds: How can the world be completed without being blown up and apocalyptically vanishing, as it does in the Christian-religious foreglow? Art attempts this completion only in ever concretely individual forms with the total envisioned as the expanding particular, while religion seeks an at least utopian completion in the totality and posits even the well-being of the individual cause entirely in the *totum*, in the 'I make all things new'.[6]

Expressing the inner entelechy of the present, art anticipates its future development and experiments with its possibilities. Thus it goes beyond the existent and creates the nothingness of freedom in which alone Being can reveal itself. However, art manifests no more than the immanent presence of Being. To assert its transcendence it must await further word. "Further word," because the power for such an assertion lies not in the aesthetic consciousness itself, and because, as we shall see later, it can only be verbally transmitted. To view existence as essentially *dependent* on Being requires an altogether different attitude.

How then can the artist adopt this attitude and create works that are genuinely *religious, that is, explicitly manifesting the transcendent?* Elsewhere I have shown that the representation of a so-called religious subject is by no means sufficient to achieve this goal.[7] Any religious claim made for madonnas by such painters as Raphael and Parmigianino must remain hazardous. While not excluding a transcendent interpretation, their work does not *require* one: it is self-sufficiently aesthetic. The inadequacy of a topical criterion renders the question all the more urgent: What distinguishes genuine religious art, say Angelico's paintings or Bach's oratorios, from other masterworks dealing with similar subjects and yet not qualifying as unambiguously religious?

Before presenting my own view, I must dispose of yet another popular answer. Religious art can definitely not be described as an expression of the artist's religious commitment. Aside from the fact that any theory which posits the work of art as "expressing" a previously completed feeling fails to account for the intrinsic quality of the creation itself, in this particular instance the theory conflicts even with commonly known facts. Some religious artists were genuinely religious persons. Such was clearly the case with Fra Angelico and Bach. But others, such as Perugino, were not, or not obviously, devout. Not the quality of the artist's preceding feelings determines the religious nature of his work, but his ability to probe and articulate the religious attitude in the creative process itself. Such an exploration undoubtedly requires some previous acquaintance with that attitude, but it is by no means necessary that the artist himself be religiously committed when he takes up brush, pen, or chisel. The specific feelings expressed in the work of art are both articulated *and constituted* in the creative process itself. Besides, no religious person would accept the equation of religion with feelings, pious or other. Usually he distrusts feelings, however uplifting, cultivated and explored for their own sake, because he knows feelings to be his own and, as such, clearly distinct from the transcendent with which his mind is chiefly occupied. Only few devout souls were able, as Fra Angelico, to translate their entire aesthetic concern into an act of worship. The grain of truth I detect in the "religious expression" theory is that no artist can create genuine religious art, unless he is seriously acquainted with, and works out of, a transcendent vision. But an acquaintance of this nature, however intensive, is clearly insufficient for the creation of religious *art*. Many devout souls write, sing, or paint what they are unable to contain within themselves. But only aesthetic sensitivity is able to convert such pious expressions into artistic creations.

It hardly needs saying that a definition of religious art by its effect—the ability to provoke pious feelings—is even less adequate. Aside from the practical difficulty of distinguishing such feelings from related ones such as the sublime, the noble, the morally uplifting, and so forth, we face the uncomfortable fact that what religiously inspires one person may fail to inspire others. Is the effect enough to render the object religious? The degree to which this effect depends on the setting should give us pause. Most people are religiously affected by art that is associated with worship. Thus they may be piously moved by the converted lyrics of a German drinking song known in its sacred version as "A Mighty Fortress Is Our God." An identical composition sounds sacred when played on an organ in a church and "profane" when performed on a piano in a saloon. A definition by association inevitably fails, because different cultures use different sounds and images to represent the sacred.

Symbols of Transcendence

Ready now to risk a definition of my own, I must reiterate the crucial
yet insufficiently recognized fact that art can no longer be religious in
a historical culture as it is in an archaic one. The difference results not
from the new aesthetic standards required by different cultural expression; it affects the very *essence* of art. To the archaic mind art belongs
mainly to the area of what is more real and powerful than the ordinary.
But this area does not stand separate from the rest of life, and the notion of transcendence which fulfills such an important function in later
religion does not apply. Whether the cave drawings of Altamira were
magical, religious, or artistic is a moot question, since such distinctions had not yet been formulated. Only later does the distinction between the more and the less important require a *distinct sphere* of
being—the realm of the sacred. At this stage religion proper (for
which archaic man has neither word nor concept) originates. Religious
symbols gradually assume a specific quality which distinguishes them
from other symbolic forms. All art continues to be determined by the
religious world view. Yet, in addition, artists feel the need to create a
consciously religious art in order to articulate aesthetically what is no
longer the *exclusive* domain of art. Since this forces them to express
what has come to be recognized as ultimately inexpressible, they must
rely heavily on the particular vision through which their culture views
transcendence. In the final analysis this will always require words, for
words alone can denote *explicitly* what surpasses ordinary visible or
auditory signs. Thus religious art work becomes increasingly dependent upon verbal initiation. It thereby also adopts a more esoteric character, in that it refuses to disclose its meaning to the doctrinally unini-
tiated. On the other hand, to fellow members of a religious tradition
that meaning may be conveyed directly through aesthetic symbols.
Visual and even auditory images can evoke the well-known message
without words. Primitive Christians recognized the emblem of the fish
as a symbol of Christ as easily as the educated today identify the half-
naked old man with book and lion as St. Jerome. Yet to the outsider
such symbolic reminders of verbal initiation must remain cryptic. Only
a Buddhist or a student of Buddhist culture directly perceives the Buddha in the position of the hand of a sculpture, or the Bodhisattva in the
oval-shaped flame around the body.[8] Even so, we must remember,
conventional symbols alone do not suffice to render a work of art

genuinely religious. An alabaster vase may have saved many a risqué painting of a female nude from direct censorship. But more is needed to convert it into a *religious* portrait of Mary Magdalen. Nevertheless, symbols or words (e.g., the title of a composition for instrumental music), however insufficient, are indispensable to achieve the transition from the implicitly to the exlicitly sacred.

If the preceding considerations are basically sound, then there can be no single characteristic of religious expression. For art can appear religious only within a specific cultural context with particular religious doctrines. Symbols that are by *their very nature* religious cannot exist, even though their existence has been a common assumption in much art criticism. To be sure, certain symbols occur more frequently to the religious mind than others. Thus light, expanding space, silence quite commonly express a transcendent reality. Yet they are neither indispensable nor exclusively religious. Indeed, no symbol is. Even those which have been introduced for their religious power may lose their expressiveness and freeze into mere artistic conventions, no more significant than the allegorical symbols (alabaster vase, book and lion) that clutter religious iconography. On the other hand, the repeated use of a particular symbol may reinforce its religious expressiveness. What is transmitted through the centuries is more apt to suggest a divinely revealed origin. But tradition can do no more than predispose a device to be used as a religious symbol. Its actual expressiveness depends on the aesthetic talent of the individual artist who uses it.

Of course, religious attitudes display some common features. But since those features are not intrinsically aesthetic and may be artistically translated into a variety of forms, they cannot be considered to be distinctive of religious *art as such*. It is safe to assert, I believe, that religious art tends to display the inadequacy of the aesthetic form with respect to its transcendent content. But this inadequacy may be conveyed in a number of ways. One of the simplest and oldest modes of expressing the transcendence of the referent with respect to the image consists in the adoption of outsized proportions. The colossal masses of Egyptian pyramids evoke another, superhuman world. So do Mexican temples, Babylonian reliefs, and many Buddhist statues.[9]

But the presence of the inexpressible may be equally evoked by the fragmentary character of the work. The unfinished easily suggests that the subject in the end exceeded the artist's creative power. Ernst Bloch even ascribes the incompleteness of such masterpieces as Beethoven's late quartets, Goethe's Faust, a number of Michelangelo's sculptures, and Leonardo's paintings to an unusual awareness of eschatological transcendence on the part of their creators.

> In the faith of Exodus and of the Kingdom totality cannot be totally transforming and disruptive, utopian. Before this totality all Being as it has become must appear fragmentary.[10]

Even technically "finished" religious works often display suggestions of incompleteness. At least in the West with its strong emphasis on transcendence, artistic expressions of the sacred tend to remain open-ended. This is one reason why Renaissance architecture, so complete in its self-contained perfection, may impress one as less religious than Gothic. Rightly or wrongly we even judge non-Christian art by the same standards. Thus the more elementary style of "archaic" Greek sculpture appears more religiously inspired than the pure classical beauty of the fifth century. Similarly, the empty space of a Chinese landscape radiates infinity by minimizing form. In the famous Japanese Oxcard pictures form progressively vanishes, leaving the viewer in the last one with nothing but a blank meditation on Nirvana. Even in architecture this effect of transcendent emptiness has been pursued and obtained. When the visitor to the Borobudur temple in Java, after ascending along an endless repetition of Buddha statues, finally emerges at the top plateau, nothing awaits him but open space. The evocation of empty space has also been a favorite symbol of some religious painters in the West. Giovanni Bellini's beautiful Madonna del Prato stands all by herself in a space of her own detached from her surroundings. Perugino's meditative spaciousness separates his sacred figures from one another, turning them inward upon an inner presence.

Inadequacy is also conveyed by the distorted figures of Grünewald's "Crucifixion" and Servaes's "Stations of the Cross," or by the elongated bodies of Van der Weyden and El Greco (with whom it tends to become a purely formal principle). Even indeterminateness and ambiguity may be religiously expressive. The vine mosaics on the vaults of Santa Costanza in Rome could be merely decorative designs or devalued pagan symbols. But to one who considers them to be Christian (which they are [11]) their indeterminate character provides them with a religious force and richness seldom found in more precisely defined symbols. Polymorphous, open-ended symbols reveal several

layers of meaning from which the transcendent slowly and almost naturally emerges. Is it not their very discreetness that makes the shepherds, fishes, and vines of primitive Christian art religiously so much
more inspiring than the rigidly defined allegories or conventional symbols of later times?

A similar effect of insufficiency is frequently obtained by the use of
the artistic material. Such, I take it, was the aim of Baroque sculptors
and architects under whose hands marble ceases to be marble and, in
ever expanding forms and shapes, moves towards infinity. In the
famous Bavarian churches of Banz and Vierzehnheiligen matter becomes fugitive and almost spiritual in a succession of continuously
regressing planes. The Baroque vault transcends its architectonic place
altogether and, along receding frescoes of religious apotheoses (most
spectacularly in the Gesù and San Ignazio), soars into a groundless
beyond. Even the elliptic form of those churches suggests a circle
breaking through its own enclosure. Of course, all too often the original inspiration degenerates into a bravura display. But the very idea of
forcing the rigorously contained space of Renaissance art into an infinitely expanding celestial vault leaves no doubt about its religious origin.

All the preceding forms evoke transcendence in a negative way, that
is, by emphasizing the inadequacy of the form. Yet there are also positive symbols of the divine. One of them, so universally known that it
seems to be almost a natural symbol of the divine, is light. We find it
in reliefs of the revolutionary Egyptian king Akhenaton, in statuary of
the Iranian religion of Ahura-Mazda, in the sun and moon pyramids of
Teotihuacan, in Byzantine mosaics and in Baroque chiaroscuro paintings. Though the opposition between divine light and profane darkness
superabounds in the Hebrew and Christian Scriptures,[12] its specific use
in our artistic tradition has mainly been determined by Neoplatonic
sources. For Plotinus light refracts the spiritual in the material world.
After having been adapted to Christian theology by Pseudo-Dionysius,
the light motive came to hold a primary place in the development of
Western art. Mosaics which reflected the light in chipped stones
proved to be a particularly appropriate medium for celebrating God's
majesty. The Italian primitives adopted the golden background of Byzantine mosaics in their paintings. Barely had the gold disappeared
when the dramatic contrast of light and dark, more expressive of the
religious turmoil of the modern age, reintroduced the religious light

symbolism. Baroque artists flooded their sacred figures with light in the midst of darkness. For many this soon became a purely formal principle. But with deeply religious masters such as Ribera and Rembrandt, the new technique led to unprecedented religious effects. Like marble under the hand of the Baroque sculptor, light ceased to be a material entity: it became totally spiritual.

Neoplatonist philosophy inspired a number of other devices, such as the frontal position of the figures, their immobility and lack of perspective, the absence of individual resemblance, by means of which religious artists attempted to overcome the transitory, accidental world and to capture the permanent essence of a hidden, spiritual universe. Thus Byzantine images were more abstract symbols than concrete representations.[13] By the simplicity of its types, the purity of its lines, and the quiet of its harmonies the Christian art of the Eastern Empire majestically evoked the eternal cosmos. We find similar tendencies in the static, depersonalized representation of Buddha statues. Whether in the hieratic mode of Siam or in the simple one of Ceylon, the Enlightened One always appears as having overcome individual personhood.[14] Even Western art, so much more hospitable to the historical and the unique, attempted to suspend time in order to convey transcendence. Thus in early Nativity scenes the figures appear frozen into immobility at the moment when the eternal entered into time. The gestures of the shepherds and angels arrested in a Sleeping Beauty-like effect impress upon the viewer that time has stood still.[15]

Of course, the very notion of absolute transcendence creates a constant tension in the development of religious art, which periodically explodes in iconoclastic movements. They left a permanent stamp upon the religious aesthetics of Judaism and Islam. Apprehensive of expressing the invisible in visible forms, those radically monotheistic faiths preferred to renounce all iconography and instead to concentrate on the word and the more abstract forms of music and architecture. In Christianity faith in the Incarnation always prevailed over the distrust of finite forms. Thus after the onslaught of the Isaurian emperors in the ninth century, the Fourth Council of Constantinople decreed: "It is conformed to reason and the oldest tradition that the icons, since they refer to the principals themselves, in a derivative way be honored and adored, even as the sacred book of the holy Gospels and the image of the precious cross are venerated." [16] In this instance victory led to a total restoration. The iconoclasm of sixteenth-century Calvinism led to different results and occasioned the development of a purely secular art. Yet even this radical revolution did not mark the end of a Christian iconography in Calvinist countries, but spurred the religious imagination into exploring new possibilities. Driven out of the church, iconic art went into book and print, less liable to become objects of "idolatrous" veneration and more subject to the close supervision of the written word. The more literalist exegesis following in the trail of the *sola scriptura* principle favored philological information over mystical inspiration and, in religious iconography, replaced mannerism by naturalism. In great religious masters such as Rembrandt it inspired an unprecedented search for inner truth. In others this search could, and indeed did, become secularized into psychology. But in Rembrandt psychological truth itself became in fact expressive of a deeper, religious inwardness.[17] In his last years the Dutch master had become so intimately familiar with the biblical scenes of his daily meditation that he dispensed with the stories altogether and directly painted their inner impact.

The New Meaning of Religious Art

The principles which we have just developed cannot be simply "applied" to modern art. The profound secularization of our age makes it questionable whether art can still be called religious even in that minimum sense in which all authentic art of the past could be considered "potentially religious." Karsten Harries describes the change as follows:

> Modern art thus appears either as an attempt to restore to man lost immediacy or as a search for absolute freedom. In either case man has given up his attempts to discover meaning in the world of objects; if there is to be meaning it must have its foundation in something beyond that world. But it is no longer possible to give definite content to this transcendence.[18]

Though I have reservations about the pessimistic conclusion, a great deal of evidence supports the basic premises. What, then, is so different about the new era?

Nothing perhaps better illustrates the nature of the aesthetic revolution than Cézanne's innovations in perspective and pictorial representation. Characteristic is the absence of any reference beyond the artistic image. The connection with the world outside the work of art has been severed. Space ceases to serve its traditional function: to relate the various forms to the viewer and to one another. What we witness now is the exact opposite of the Baroque art where expansive quality, that is, the ability of form to point beyond itself, played a more important role than inner consistency. Even the heaviest marble and the darkest color became transparent in their power to surpass the actual representation. Baroque objects expanded in time as well as in space: they told a story.[19] Though much of this narrative quality was lost in subsequent Neoclassicism, Realism, and Impressionism, the referential quality remained. Represented objects continued to be unified in the one perspective determined by the viewer's eye.

Cézanne reversed that principle in painting. Similar though less conspicuous changes transformed sculpture, music, literature, and architecture. The artistic representation of the new era became detached from the viewer and the listener, and came to be enclosed in its own independent space and meaning. Not how things look *to the viewer,* or how music sounds *to the listener,* determines the artistic creation, but how forms and tone combinations appear *in themselves.* Of course, the phrase "appear in themselves" is contradictory, since form and tone always appear to a perceiving subject. Still I find no more appropriate expression to convey the modern artist's disregard of the viewer's or listener's predisposition. Pictorial objects continue to appear in a particular perspective, of course, but not in one that is immediately accessible to the viewer. Tones are still received with specific expectations of harmony, but the composer makes no effort to meet those expectations. The abolition of a subjective viewpoint was entailed by the disappearance of a unified connection between the various parts of the painting, composition, or narrative. Partial units stand by themselves, often juxtaposed in their own particular perspective, or else connected by fragmentary perspectives.

When Cézanne replaced contours by color patches, the visual image (which was soon to become a mere color combination) solidified into an alien and opaque reality. Eventually, it came to stand by itself, independent of the viewer and of related images, and ceased to refer beyond itself in space and time. We find ourselves in a *presence* without history and without world.[20] I should add: and without transcendence. Contemporary art merely articulates modern man's feeling toward the world. Things simply *are,* indifferent to the human observer, self-contained in an inhuman solitude. Only in recent years has literature attempted an equally radical negation of humanness and coherence in the so-called antinovel which is, in fact, an antinarrative. In architecture nonreferential self-sufficiency mostly took the form of an unprecedented emphasis on the material of the construction, the specific qualities of brick, stone, or wood, at the expense of the aptitude to receive and orient the visitor according to his needs. This appears most clearly in religious buildings. Worshipers now find themselves in churches with neither front nor center, where a multitude of vectors intersect at various places. In such an inhospitable space each man is left to discover his own Orient, to create his own perspective, and to explore his own feelings.

The new concept of spatial construction, it is sometimes claimed, allows man to find *himself* instead of having a particular perspective forced upon him. This is all too true, for nothing in this alien space refers beyond the actually given. The only transcendence is that of matter itself. Here we see combined the two tendencies of modern art according to Harries's description: an attempt to restore lost immediacy and a search for absolute freedom. The purely immediate imposes no restrictions upon the pure choice. In the absence of any beyond but that of matter itself man has no choice but to become his own transcendence. Thus total objectivism results in pure subjectivism. "The attempt to replace the world with constructions that have their foundation in freedom alone can in the end not be distinguished from the opposite striving to have artistic creation by nothing more than spontaneous expression." [21] Total unsituatedness traps the self within a closed world of mere possibilities. But since freedom must be grounded in, and limited by, consistent actuality, *mere* possibility allows no genuine freedom. Kierkegaard who defined despair as lack of possibility, was right in diagnosing a self that is *mere* possibility as a self in despair. For *mere* possibility is no *real* possibility. We may also learn from Kierkegaard how such despair is essentially religious: the negation of a consistent actuality originates in the refusal to accept a unifying transcendent foundation. [22]

Nowhere does the nihilist quality of absolute freedom appear more clearly than in contemporary literature. Here the loss of transcendence undermines the continuity of the time structure itself and thereby the very essence of the narrative. The world becomes reduced to a juxtaposition of unrelated objects, and existence to a succession of incoherent episodes. Frank Kermode has shown how the absence of inner connection between the stages of existence is symbolized in the modern storyteller's inability to find an appropriate ending.[23] But, as Virginia Woolf once remarked, if there are no beginnings and endings, there are no stories. Life then becomes a circle that turns around itself. French modern writers have followed this state of mind to its ultimate consequences. In Robbe-Grillet time itself has been reduced to a mere sequence of independent moments without inner coherence, while Beckett's entire work may be read as an expression of discontinuous selfhood in which personal identity disintegrates into a series of isolated states. Anglo-American literature has rarely followed this path into absurdity. Nonetheless, the present vogue of literary formalism reveals a similar state of nontranscendent ultimacy. Despairing of modern man's ability to attain ultimate significance, writers have increasingly turned to form as an end in itself. Destitute of content, form becomes a last barrier against chaos in an uncentered universe. Yet literature cannot dispense with content. So the writer finds himself forced to write *about* form rather than *with* it.[24] Verbal signs are juxtaposed in a way that excludes a consistent model of reality. Language appears in the telling itself and develops its own patterns of meaning. Though its referential quality cannot be eliminated, modern writers have gone as far as possible in loosening the connection with a coherently real world.

As long as man continues to define himself as self-transcending— and there are strong indications that he does, albeit in the negative way of one who fails to achieve transcendence—the absence of any beyond causes in fact a fundamental disorientation. Yet could the opaque objectivity of modern art itself not offer a rest from the desperate struggle for orientation? Does its very immediacy not present a respite from freedom? Nonfigurative art revives the old dream of a new immediacy.

> Sometimes when the strains of survival slacken, we may again, as when we were children, begin to see the sensuous and its structures as windowless monads. Then the radiant and vivid values of the sensuous are enjoyed for their own sake, satisfying a primal, fundamental need.[25]

The immediacy is real enough, but I doubt whether it suffices to render art religiously significant.

The expecting openness which modern art requires has been compared to the "immobilization before life," the "prolonged attention" characteristic of the religious attitude.[26] Few who have undergone the full impact of such powerful abstractionists as Rothko, Kline, and Kandinski would rule out such an interpretation. Yet it would be confusing to call their works religious in the same sense as Duccio and Van der Weyden. While a religious viewing is a possibility with the former, with the latter it is a necessity. Great abstract art in painting, music, and sculpture may provide the openness in which transcendence may be rediscovered; it does not show the transcendent itself.

Similar claims may be made with even more ground of some expressionist and postexpressionist works. Such masters of modern agony as Arshile Gorky, Francis Bacon, Willem de Kooning, and Germaine Richier undoubtedly raise questions of ultimate meaning. To depict the horror of a centerless universe is to question the viability of a world without transcendence. Again such visions of doom *may be* interpreted religiously, but they need not be and, in fact, they were mostly inspired by the artist's own despair of a religious integration. They present images of insufficiency which may invite the viewer to an inner vision of his own but which contribute no content to that vision themselves. In this they differ from the great religious artists of the past who did more than raise a question: they opened up a positive vision of the sacred. Only by imposing his own religious attitude on the artist's work can the viewer perceive contemporary expressionist art as religious. Religious art of the past left no such freedom of interpretation. To enter into Bach's Oratorios or Van der Weyden's Depositions even a totally secular person has no choice but to adopt temporarily the artist's transcendent vision. For a brief moment the artist forces him to share his own religious world view. The contemporary artist leaves the initiative to the spectator.

The ambiguity of modern art with respect to the sacred is significant for a situation in which man has mostly lost the direct experience of the sacred. Rarely does he attain more than a sense of absence, a silence, or, at best, an inner space in which transcendence may become manifest again. We are reminded of Heidegger's word that in a destitute time such as ours poets no longer speak of the holy, or of the gods, but only of the traces they left.[27] The sacred function of art, then, may be no more than to create the vacuum in which man is able to perceive transcendence. The position of modern art is essentially ambiguous toward the sacred.

Is this to say that no sacred art exists in our time? To see the absurdity of such a conclusion it suffices to think of Matisse's chapel in Vence, of some of Manzù's sculptures, of most of Rouault's paintings and, above all, of Messiaen's and Penderecki's sacred compositions. Those works demand an unambiguously religious interpretation, if one is to enter into their meaning at all. Nor can they be dismissed as cultural leftovers from an earlier age: their creators all pioneered in their own medium. Still, though the modern significance of their work is beyond doubt, they can hardly be considered the most representative artists of our time. More attuned to the religious climate of our age are those abstract and expressionist artists whom we discussed earlier. A particularly interesting problem is created by pure abstractionists attempting to create explicitly religious art, such as Barnett Newman did in his "Stations of the Cross" or Rothko in his Houston Chapel. Here the religious ambiguity of modern art stands fully exposed, and with it the need for a return to the original determination of language. Without the title no one would be able to recognize those works as definitely religious. In a cultural tradition where the symbols of faith are well known, representational artists seldom feel the need for such verbal professions. With the exception of music (essentially a nonrepresentational art) the title plays no decisive role in determining the religious nature of an iconic work. The long hair, the vase, and the somewhat disheveled appearance of an attractive woman immediately alerts the viewer that he stands in the presence of St. Mary Magdalen. Everyone knows the story. Of course, a title under an abstract painting may be arbitrary or even deliberately misleading, but no more so than the cultic symbols or even the entire subject in a traditional work lacking in genuine religious inspiration. We are reminded once again that language (or iconic symbols that ultimately require verbal interpretation) is indispensable but not sufficient to the creation of religious art. When an art form severs its ties from the iconic tradition, the call for the word reappears in its pristine urgency. To obey this call today is no more arbitrary than it was to the original image makers of a religious tradition and than it has been to religious composers of all times. It illustrates once more that to the religious mind the primeval relation to the transcendent is established by a revelation of the word.

6

Alienation and Redemption of the Self in Time and Memory

Intelligence as it recollects the intuition, places the content of feeling in its own inwardness—in a space and time of its own. Representation is this recollected intuition.

HEGEL

In the distention of time man experiences perhaps the most fundamental estrangment from himself. Men and women of every age have been deeply concerned about the transitoriness of life. The experience that what *was* no longer is, and that what *is* will soon no longer be, including one's very existence, creates a need of redemption from the annihilating impact of time, expressed by Nietzsche's Zarathustra: "To redeem those who lived in the past and to recreate all 'it was' into a 'thus I willed it'—that alone should I call redemption." [1] Not surprisingly, it is above all from this constant passage into otherness and nonbeing that religion offers salvation. In the following pages I propose to investigate how the Christian vision achieves this goal not by abolishing time but by interiorizing it through the function of memory.

Mythical Repetition and Religious Eternity

Much has been written about the cyclical repetitions in which myth and ritual recall the foundational events of life and thereby convey permanence and necessity to the transitory phases of life. Returning time here overcomes the passage of time. By being reversible the so-called mythical past in fact ceases to be a past. It becomes an absolute time, not preceded by a more remote past or followed by a future, in which "the end is like the beginning and the beginning like the end, a kind of eternity, since it is not a sequence of time but only one time".[2] Religion, to the extent that it suceeds in detaching itself from purely mythical thought, attempts to replace this "kind of eternity" by a real one.

Meanwhile the purely mythical presentation already displays an important feature of such religions as Judaism and Christianity, namely, that the access to a *permanent* present must be found not in the present but in the past. The myth returns to the past in order to establish the present. This does not mean that the myth always attempts *to return the past* (this is certainly not the case for evil), but at least that all important events, including the negative and painful ones, require a foundation in the past in order to become meaningful and thereby manageable. The past alone presents a wholeness which the continuing present lacks: in its completeness the flux of becoming reaches permanence.

It appears to be the concept of eternity which distinguishes advanced religions, even those which grant time itself a redemptive role, from the archaic myth with respect to temporal succession. In referring to it as a distinctive principle, I do not mean that eternity is clearly separated from time. Indeed, such a separation seldom occurs. Usually eternity itself appears as an extension of time, but a unique one that is no longer subject to succession and development. Nor are the relations between this eternity and ordinary temporality identical or even similar in all cases. What we find is rather a variety of symbolic representations of eternity and of its relation to time. Thus while Vendantic Hinduism achieves redemption through a negation of time as principle of separation and fragmentation, Judaism and Christianity attribute a permanent meaning to the passage of time itself. In the following reflections I shall concern myself primarily with the Christian view.

But this cannot be understood without some reference to Greek philosophy and Hebrew faith.

Clearly there is no "Greek" position on time, but only a long development. Nevertheless, it is safe to claim, I believe, that in general Greek philosophy does not ignore or abolish time, as some religious philosophies of the East do. While Milesian "philosophy" was still full of mythology, Parmenides' thought signals a drastic and mostly successful attempt to abandon the mythic view altogether. In any event, the demythologizing process which he initiated continued to downgrade the status of time with respect to eternity, until it came to rest in the aesthetic balance of Plato's theory. The key idea which separated myth from philosophy appears to have been that what is temporal, and therefore transitory, cannot ultimately determine what is universal, and therefore permanent.

> While the myth illumines the meaning of reality by telling a story, philosophy, precisely because it aims at being scientific and universal, takes its distance from time. It interprets what occurs against the horizon of what does not occur but what *is*, that is, by means of timeless principles.[3]

However, Greek philosophy does not ignore or abolish time, as the religions of the East do. Though the suppression of temporality was not entirely unknown—for Parmenides all becoming is illusory—generally the Greeks attributed a positive significance to time. The eternal, far from excluding the temporal, founds it. Eternity conveys the permanence and necessity without which time would remain wholly amorphous. Thus for Plato time, the image of eternity, is also its only gate to access. Only through the essentially temporal process of *recollection* can the soul regain its original dwelling place, the eternal kingdom of the ideas. Still the two realms remain essentially distinct. For the process of recollecting, though it occurs in time, leads beyond time. It aims at the atemporal at the end of time, in which all succession ceases and being regains its pristine permanence. The distinction of the temporal and the eternal order is essential for understanding the true meaning of the immortality to which Plato devotes so much attention. It is a new mode of being resulting from a transformation of existence, not from an addition of time. This qualitative distinction between time and eternity will remain. In fact to Epicurus and his disciples true eternity must be attained exclusively by a certain manner of living the present, not by an infinitely protracted temporality.[4]

Yet Plato or later Greek philosophers never entirely integrated time with eternity. The two would remain juxtaposed, until time itself, mainly under the influence of Plotinus's philosophy, became the form of internal duration. We must not forget that even for Plato time was still primarily *cosmological,* an intrinsic quality of the cosmos itself. To Gregory of Nyssa and Augustine time was primarily a psychological category. The Christian Fathers introduced yet another innovation. As heirs of Hebrew theology they regarded time as deriving a lasting significance from God's deeds in history. History thus came to interact with an eternity which they believed to be incarnated in time. The new vision does not automatically abolish the alienation of the time experience. To the Christian also the days are evil (Ephesians 5:16), and time must be redeemed before it can be accepted. But redemption can no longer consist in an escape from temporality, for "only through time time is conquered." [5] The Christian's aim in the struggle between eternity and time can only be the victory of eternity in time, not the abolition of time. [6]

Nor can he be satisfied with a historical salvation, for the time of history is the past, and salvation takes place in the present. The Christian then must *re-present* the past. The events of the Incarnation remain historically unique: they belong to the past and bear no repetition. Yet faith enables the believer to become contemporary with them. In doing so he becomes contemporary with his own past as well, and indeed with the entire past of history. The instant in which the eternal penetrates time, and to which the believer becomes present at his own instant of grace, marks each moment with permanent significance.

Again, such a synthesis presupposes that time be recognized as primarily a quality of the mind. Only the mind can transcend time without ceasing to be intrinsically temporal, because only the mind is able to hold on to the past and to anticipate the future. An objective succession of events cannot account for either retention or anticipation: the past would survive the present and the future would remain totally unknown. In Augustine's immortal words:

It is in you, O my mind, that I measure time.—What I measure is the impress produced in you by things as they pass and abiding in you when they have passed: and it is present. I do not measure the things themselves whose passage produced the impress; it is the impress that I measure when I measure time. [7]

Yet in remembering the past I do more than merely retain it: I recreate it and give it a new mode of being instead of the one which it lost when it ceased to be present.

Since the studies of Husserl and Bergson we have come to realize fully how erroneous the empiricist conception of memory is, according to which the remembered past is no more than a series of "reproduced" impressions, with the representation of time conveyed entirely by the succession of ideas itself. (The original, unadorned version of this theory appears in Hume's *Treatise on Human Nature*.) Memory never copies the past: it constitutes it as past by breathing new life into a bygone reality, and by placing it in a wholly new context. Rather than being the present depending on the past, memory is the past recreated in and by the present. "In memory we stand in the Now, in the object of memory we stand in the past Now." [8] A remembrance, then, is not a present "image" or "copy" of the past, but its *represented* actuality. [9] Memory mysteriously revives the past in a new time and a new space. In remembering I move from the outer space of perception to the inner space of the mind. Similarly, I retemporalize events, not merely by remembering them *as past,* but also, and especially, by withdrawing them from the original succession of actual perception. I can remember events without having to recall all the circumstances which surrounded them; I can lift them out of the chain of cause and effect; I can even invert their order of appearance. And I do so constantly. The time of memory, Husserl observed, differs qualitatively from the time of perception: it is an inner, or "immanent" time. [10] This interiorization is clearly expressed in the German *Erinnerung,* which led Hegel to consider memory the first stage of the internalizing process in which the mind construes aesthetic and religious representations. [11] Memory conveys an intimate quality to the past which allows it to surpass the mere objectivity of events and to become part of the self's own subjective life. Even as it contracts the world into an inner space does memory recollect history into autobiography. In its purifying crucible representations are transformed into the soul's own substance.

The Pitfalls of Memory

Still memory alone cannot completely undo the destructive work of time. The past can never be relived in its immediacy, and much of it is irretrievably lost. The mind's own temporal perspective prevents it from ever exhaustively understanding its past.[12] "The individual human who recalls the past and comprehends its meaning was not the being who constituted the past in the first place."[13] Moreover, to remember the past is not yet to redeem it. Clearly, not every memory is liberating. Psychoanalysis would be a less complex art, if a simple recall of a traumatic experience would cure the patient. Indeed, often it is the oppressive weight of certain memories which drove the patient to seek treatment in the first place. Many who suffered through war or concentration camp never knew how to unburden themselves of all too vivid memories that continue to haunt their present. Of course, the person who is neurotically obsessed by the past does not really *remember* the past, but rather attempts to *repeat* it and, in reliving the painful events of his past, to attain a new ending different from the one he cannot accept. This is entirely true. Yet even full remembrance does not heal the wounds of the past. Remembrance alone offers no cure. Nor does it offer religious salvation. Persistent memories of past evil, suffered or perpetrated, far from being redemptive have gradually drained the faith from many a believer's heart.

Moreover, if memory can disturb the present, it may also obliterate the future. Remembering the past may fascinate one into forgetfulness of the present. The remembering attitude reduces the real to reflection in which "enterprises . . . lose the name of action" (*Hamlet* III, 1). Memory itself then assumes the three dimensions of past, present, and future, but projects them all into the past. Thus I come to remember the present and future instead of creating them. The hard edge of actuality which solely conveys the full sense of the real is softened into the remembrance of a dream. It is the evaporation of the present which Kierkegaard describes in *Either/Or:*

> There is nothing more dangerous to me than remembering. The moment I have remembered some life-relationship, that moment it ceased to exist.—A remembered life-relation has already passed into eternity and has no more temporal interest.[14]

Already Rousseau was acquainted with this "romantic" reflectivity and analyzes it in his *Confessions:*

> I do not know how to see what is before my eyes; I can only see clearly in retrospect, it is only in memories that my mind can work. I have neither feeling nor understanding for anything that is said or done or that

happens before my eyes. All that strikes me is the external manifestation. But afterwards it all comes back to me, I remember the place and the time, the tone of voice and look, the gesture and situation, nothing escapes me.[15]

We find a similar idea expressed in Jean Paul's *Titan:*

> If here below fiction could become fact, and our pastoral poetry pastoral life and every dream a day,—ah, even then would desire still remain enhanced only, not fulfilled: the higher reality would only beget a higher poetry, and higher remembrances and hopes; in *Arcadia* we should pine after Utopia; and on every sun we should see an unfathomable starry heaven retiring before us, and we should—sigh as we do here.[16]

Jean Paul introduces the utopian element of the future as well as the idyllic element of the past. But the one time that is eliminated is the present.

The romantic mind has always found itself mysteriously attracted to the silent realm of memory where present gestures freeze into returning rhythms and actual sounds into repeated echoes. There, as in the strange castle of Resnais's film *Last Year in Marienbad,* we wander aimlessly around, shadows in a past that never *was,* but that consists of projections reversed into the time of remembrance. When the present is experienced as *dejà vu,* each new sensation is prefaced by "une fois de plus. . . ." Proust has inimitably exploited the poetic potential of those instants of timelessness in which we remember the present while reliving the past. Kierkegaard rightly considered such an attitude to be essentially aesthetic. Every artist re-presents (and re-creates) past experience. He consciously re-enacts what he lived but incompletely understood. Through this creative interpretation of his memories he achieves a new, symbolic present. From his endeavors we learn an important lesson. The self can only be remembered. It is present merely as the re- of representation which, uniting all experiences in time and space, transcends them in a timeless past [17]—"that darkness of sleep which is the past, and is the self." [18]

Yet the aesthetic memory is not redemptive of the present. And this is precisely what religion claims for its own way of remembering. How then can memory ever become salutary and introduce the permanence of eternity into the passage of time? Augustine who first disclosed the full religious significance of memory raises the question:

But where in my memory do You abide, Lord, where in my memory do You abide? What resting place have you claimed as Your own, what sanctuary built for Yourself? [19]

Experiences come and go, and memory is the awareness of their constant destruction. Yet it is in the double awareness of this continuous passage of the self into nothingness and of the permanence of the remembered self that the religious mind attains the still point where the passing comes to rest and the past is forever preserved. Such a · transcending of time is achieved not by the mere reminiscence of the past but by a new perspective on the present.

From Remembrance to Recollection

Religious recollection consists in a conversion, via the past, toward a more interior self which is no longer subject to the passage of time, because it rests in eternity. Its aim is not so much to evoke memories as to review temporal succession in its totality. By returning to the nothingness at its beginning the self places its entire history in a contingent perspective. The experience of radical historicity together with an insistent perception of lasting selfhood evoke the expectation of an atemporal present at the origin of existence.[20] Thus to know oneself is · to remember oneself, and to remember oneself entirely is to remember one's origin. At this point immanence turns into transcendence, and autobiography into confession.

The connotations of guilt and sinfulness which the modern mind detects in the term confession are not fortuitous. For to know one's past in its entirety is to know oneself as guilty. To be present to one's · whole self is to be present to oneself as both good and evil. Kierkegaard wrote that I can choose myself truly only in repentance, for only in repentance do I both accept evil as an essential part of my past and repudiate it as an estrangement of my real self.[21] Heidegger developed this idea in *Being and Time* and declared all existence in time guilty because of the essential inauthenticity of a "thrown" being.[22] Guilt is accepted in confession. To be able to confess requires the admission of one's real past, rather than of an imaginary one or of no past at all. But to condemn the self that *is*, with no other self available, is a most painful task. Temple Drake's difficulty in Faulkner's *Requiem for a Nun* is deeply symbolic. Unable to "confess," she moves back and forth between the sinful past that she has become, and her present desire to be cleansed.

The psychoanalytic method of therapy through remembrance offers some analogy to this *memoria Dei*. For here also, more than the evocation of singular memories is required. Memories alone, however much I recall, can never reveal me to myself. For to know myself fully, I would have to remember myself entirely. Only through total memory could I hope to assign to each event its due place and proportion. Yet obviously no process of recalling, however prolonged, could ever return my entire past. Instead of attempting such a futile undertaking, psychoanalytic "remembering," by uncovering and releasing characteristic yet neglected or repressed memories, aims at discovering a new, more integrating Gestalt for the past. Rather than accumulating memories, it changes the entire *perspective* of remembering.

Claude Lévi-Strauss has argued, apparently with the approval of some psychoanalysts,[23] that the unconscious, rather than being a specific set of memories (as the preconscious is), consists of a fundamental structure underlying all conscious life. If brought to consciousness by means of a myth or with the aid of an analyst, this structure integrates within a meaningful totality memories which the self was unable to accept in their unstructured presentation.[24] What is interesting in this theory is that it is not new memories but a new coherence of memories which cures. No less significant is the fact that this structure is achieved by means of mythical models. To Jung mythical archetypes are indispensable for the interpretation and expansion of dream memories. But even Freud's models of interpretation invite a recall of such ancient stories and myths (the Oedipus cycle or the myths connected with the totem cult) as the religious memory uses to reach ultimate self-understanding. To the faithful Jew no act has deeper religious significance than the remembrance of the origins. The memory of history is a religious duty, and one which extends not only to those times when Israel felt close to God, such as the Exodus event and the Sinai revelation, but also to those which seemed far away, such as the golden calf episode and, later, the holocaust. Yet more than being a sacred obligation, the remembrance of Israel's past provides the Jew with a pattern for understanding and accepting the present. Identifying with the types of the past, he finds meaning in the vicissitudes of his own existence. This remembrance becomes, of course, most effective when it is ritually revived, as in the Seder celebration. Yet also the daily presence of the biblical word provides effective patterns of meaning that allow the individual to find his own place in a sacred history. Thomas Mann disclosed a fundamental Hebrew attitude in his famous tetralogy when he presented Joseph and his family constantly searching for the appropriate historical precedents of their actions. Yet what he revealed applies to some degree to every religious consciousness. Only in the completeness of the past does the present attain final significance.

Christian remembrance has concentrated more exclusively on a single chain of events, the life, death, and resurrection of Jesus Christ. Other persons and events are magnetically centered, as prefigurations or imitations, around the God incarnate. Throughout the ages Christians have found meaning and consolation in the remembrance of Jesus' life and passion while sacramental rituals have made this life contemporary with their own. However, the christocentric nature of Christian recollection by no means restricts its function to a mere recall of the life of Christ. Since its beginnings Christian piety has regarded memory as far more than a means of establishing contact with a redeemer who lived and died in the past. Memory was, above all, the road to the inner center in which any encounter with God takes place. For that reason *all* cognition of God had to be a *memoria Dei*. This has been adequately recognized (though perhaps too easily ascribed to Platonic influences) in St. Augustine. But it already appears in those Fathers with whom the formal study of spiritual life began, the Cappadocians.[25] What one commentator concludes about the dynamisms of St. Basil's ascetical theology holds to a great extent true for all spiritual writers of East and West:

> It does appear that Basil was aware that there were such psychic forces at play in the encounter with God as led to a profound transformation of man's very character and way of being. And that these forces lay in the memory and in the diathesis [the dynamic unconscious].[26]

Religious Recollection and the Presence of History

Christians and Jews tend to distinguish historical faith from mystical piety, and the emphasis upon one or the other has been one of the divisive issues between Catholics and Protestants. Yet the distinction between personal recollection and historical memory need not be exclusive. One inevitably leads to the other, as appears clearly in St.

Augustine. The autobiographical states remembered in the *Soliloquies* are recollected as stages of God's grace in the *Confessions,* and then again assumed into sacred history in *The City of God.*[27] Augustine progresses from personal to historical recollection. The ordinary course runs in the opposite direction. The recollection of sacred history precedes, and usually initiates, the *reditus in seipsum.*

Nor is the religious recollection of history restricted to particular "sacred" events. All events of history are interwoven: if one can be recaptured, all others become ideally accessible to the present. "Each epoch is equally close to God"—and therefore also to the recollecting soul. Due to the religious perspective the study of history has taken on a unique significance for the spiritual orientation of our culture. Berdyaev suggestively evokes the mood of the Christian encounter with antiquity in his description of the Roman campagna "where historical momuments became the manifestation of nature," and where the Christian communes with a past "in which eternity is triumphant over corruption and death." [28] Yet the moment the past can be recaptured, it ceases to be mere history and turns into what Barth calls "saga," that is, history interpreted in the light of a nonhistorical, permanent presence. To Jews and Christians history never belongs entirely to the past—it remains vitally present. Even such anti-idealist iconoclasts as Marx and Nietzsche persistently continued to believe in a teleology of history.

For the same reason the representations in which religious faith expresses itself must remain permanently embedded in time: directly or indirectly, they relate to a temporal succession of events. Hegel, who keenly noticed the intrinsically historical nature of Christian symbols, claimed that their *Geschehen* may nevertheless be transcended in the timeless development of the notion.[29] Yet in such a detemporalization they undoubtedly lose their religious character. To Christians and Jews redemption remains permanently temporal and accessible only through memory. A purely existential interpretation of those faiths, such as Bultmann proposed in his early work, therefore conflicts with their very nature. Even events which no historical evidence could ever firmly establish must be *recollected* rather than *construed.* It may well be the case, as Franz Rosenzweig suggests, that no one ascended the mountain and that no one descended, yet the Sinai event, though clouded in historical darkness, remains essentially a "memorable" event.[30] Similarly, the Christian possesses no decisive historical evidence of the resurrection and very little of the "historical Jesus" in general, yet he cannot believe without what Kierkegaard called the footnote of history.

Though history is indissolubly connected with it, salvation, if the term is to retain its meaning, must take place in the present. Christians and Jews appear to experience considerable difficulty in reconciling this present with the inherent historicity of their faiths. Often they favor the latter, regarding their faith as a new, decisive epoch of history. But in doing so they reduce the redemption of time itself to a purely temporal event and sacrifice its basic meaning. In numerous polemics with the Hegelian theologians of his time Kierkegaard showed—most strongly in *Philosophical Fragments* and the subsequent *Unscientific Postscript*—how such a world-historical view ceases to be Christian or even religious. Historical events, however sacred, become redemptive only when the believer overcomes the distance of history in order to be a *contemporary* of Christ. The Hegelian view has long since been abandoned as an authentic interpretation of faith. But the same historicism reappears today in some of the so-called theologies of hope and liberation. They also constitute an attempt to redeem history by history alone. Eschatologies of the future take the place of contemporaneity. While earlier interpretations were entirely oriented toward the past of which they took the present to be the conclusion, the newer ones are exclusively directed toward a future of which the present is only the beginning. But the forward-looking memory succeeds no more in liberating man from time than the retrospective. Eliot perceptively distinguished religious recollection from either one.

> This is the use of memory:
> For liberation—not less of love by expanding
> Of love beyond desire, and so liberation
> From the future as well as the past. . . .[31]

The religious interiorization of time in memory is a deeply personal achievement directed at one's own past as much as at history. For this pious remembrance of one's life the term "recollection" with its connotation of interiority is particularly appropriate. The German *Erinnerung* conveys a sense of inwardness to all remembrance. Yet in religious recollection this inwardness becomes primary. Beyond being a search for an archetypal past, recollection is an attempt to return to the center of existence from which the distention of time irresistibly removes me.[32]

, Only if through this past man succeeds in touching a timeless present, does he consider that past redeemed and himself whole again. At that point he becomes present to his entire self and to all times. Of this moment Claudel sang:

> Rien n'a pu ou ne peut
> Etre qui ne soit à ce moment même; toutes
> Choses sont présentes pour moi. (*La Ville*)

, In it reigns the stillness at the center of all motion, that envelopes time itself:

> Not the stillness of the violin, while the note lasts,
> Not that only, but the coexistence
> Or say that the end precedes the beginning,
> And the end and the beginning were always there
> Before the beginning and after the end
> And all is always now.[33]

Recollection, the religious journey into the past, leads to the silence , behind the words. As memory releases the silent forces of the unconscious from which all speaking originates, recollection, Augustinian masters teach us, discloses the Divine Silence from which the Eternal Word springs forth. In *De Trinitate* XIV, 13, 17 St. Augustine had shown how the *memoria* contains the mind's latent knowledge both of itself and of God. To William of St. Thierry, Alexander of Hales, Bonaventure, and others in the same spiritual tradition, this meant that recollection is both the image of, and the encounter with, the mystery that gives birth to the Eternal Word in time. In Bonaventure's *Itinerarium Mentis ad Deum* we read:

> And thus through the operation of memory, it appears that the soul itself is the image of God and His likeness, so present to itself and having Him present that it receives Him in actuality and is susceptible of receiving Him in potency, and that it can also participate in Him.[34]

, In general memory has been far more to Christian spiritual writers than an ordinary "faculty" of the mind; it is the gateway to the soul's ground where God and the self coincide.

7

The Self Immortal

Personality does not demand immortality for itself, but the self does. Personality is satisfied with the eternity of the relations into which it enters and in which it is absorbed. The self has no relations, cannot enter into any, remains ever itself. Thus it is conscious of being eternal.

ROSENZWEIG

At night objects may be perceived more distinctly if we avoid focusing on them. In the same way some philosophical issues reveal their true significance only when we face them in related questions. Such an issue is the nature of the self. Philosophers have spent much attention on consciousness and on the transcendental conditions of its objective content, but they have insufficiently accounted for the nature of the subject which founds this object consciousness. Thus they have developed a notion of selfhood that appears adequate enough until we attempt to apply it to experiences that fall outside the range of ordinary object intentionality.

One set of such experiences is conceptualized in the idea of immortality. Of course, immortality itself can, from a mortal's point of view, never be called an experience. But the states of consciousness that have given rise to the belief in immortality are accessible and must be accounted for in a philosophical theory of the self. Whether man survives after death is not my primary concern in the following discussion. Even after broadening its basis, philosophy would not be able to bring this question to a definitive conclusion, I believe, and I shall have an opportunity to discuss some of the problems that continue to affect an expanded notion of the self. But even if philosophy were to find the idea of immortality without adequate support, it would still have to "justify" the origin of this idea on the basis of the experiences that led to it. This the prevalent theories of the self are unable to do. The existing, primarily empiricist theories of the self are woefully inadequate to deal not only with experiences of transcendence such as the ones that gave rise to the idea of immortality, but with almost any kind of awareness beyond the apprehension of the self in object-oriented states of consciousness.

Continuity and the Empirical Self

If immortality were merely the conclusion of a rational argument, philosophy could be satisfied with retracing the successive steps and basing its critical verdict on the logical evidence. If the latter were wanting, it could simply dismiss the case. However, the belief in life after death appears to have grown out of actual experiences far more than out of reasoning processes. Even Edward B. Tylor, who was so inclined to ascribe to the primitive mind the speculative bent of the Victorian mind, was forced to conclude on the issue of survival after death:

> The lower races claim to hold their doctrines of future life on strong tradition, direct revelation and even personal experience. To them the land of the souls is a discovered country from whose bourne many a traveler returns.[1]

Modern man is acquainted with few such experiences. Indeed, even to religious believers today the thought of a future life remains far from the center of their faith, if they do not reject it outright. Nevertheless, it would be incorrect to assume that our contemporaries remain totally deprived of intimations of permanence. In love many of us feel a suggestion of everlastingness. But few would conclude from that to the existence of a real afterlife.

In any event religious faith in survival after death should not be conceived as a primitive will to protract one's present existence beyond the grave. Religious immortality is the opposite of an expectation to continue one's present life: it is rather a call for total change. Mere survival is not at all what religious man expects. "The soul's hope has not been for more of the same, but for something altogether higher and better." [2] Indeed, the concept of an unending afterlife seems to originate in those "peak experiences" in which man perceives a glimpse of a more permanent, qualitatively different form of existence. In Greece at least it seems to have been the power to participate in the godly life through Dionysiac ecstacy which led to the belief in immortality.

The philosophical arguments against an indefinite continuance are, of course, equally formidable. To existentialist philosophers the idea of immortality basically conflicts with the very nature of man's self-understanding and the self-realization of a finite freedom. An eternity of free self-realization would turn freedom into its opposite, since over an infinity of temporal succession all possibilities must necessarily be realized. "Man can be individual and free only to the extent that he implies in his being all the possibilities of Being but does not have the time to realize and manifest them all." [3] In her philosophical novel *Tous les hommes sont mortels* Simone de Beauvoir shows that an indefinite protraction of our present existence would not only be absurd but also unbearable. Man lives his life through periods of preparation, maturity, and decline. The finitude of his achievement is essential to our conception of a life work and guides the projection of our task. The cycle of life may remain incomplete, but it cannot be indefinitely extended. If Plato and Aristotle were around today they would sadly have survived themselves.

It is the very absence, however, of a full continuity in the religious expectation of the afterlife which justifies an objective investigation of its claims. Yet, here we run instantly into another difficulty. For how much discontinuity is compatible with the continuance of *personal identity?* Most conceptions of immortality show but little concern for the consequences of what must be at the very least a basic transmutation of the person. How can the mind preserve its identity when sense perceptions and sense impulses no longer feed it? Must this not eventually result in a loss of all creative imagination and, in the end, even of memory?

H. H. Price envisions the afterlife as a world of mental pictures in which "imaging" replaces perceiving. [4] He assumes that images of organic sensations could provide what is needed to maintain an environment similar to our present one. "We can quite well image to ourselves what it feels like to be in a warm bath, even when we are not actually in one.'' [5] Yes, we can indeed, a few months or even years after we stepped out of our last bath. But can such an image-life be indefinitely continued without fresh sensory input? The possibility seems particularly remote if one conceives of the afterlife as a world in which everything possesses shape, size, color, and other qualities associated with material objects, yet where, as in Berkeley's universe, the material ''substrata'' are missing. I find it extremely difficult to conceive of colors and shapes without ever new, actual perceptions.

On the other hand, one cannot but sympathize with Price's concern to maintain conditions as similar as possible to the ones prevailing in the present world. For how could life in a bodiless state be considered the same as it was in an embodied existence, unless some corporeal orientation remains after death? Could personal identity survive even a total disruption of one's habitual bodily states? ''It is past belief that if the body of anyone of us were suddenly changed into that of a shark or an octopus, and placed in the ocean, his personality could, for more than a very short time if at all, survive intact so radical a change of environment and of bodily form.'' [6] Can a person remain the *same* without a body? Can he remain the *same* with another ''spiritualized'' body? Prior to a discussion of those problems of identity we must at least in a provisional way settle the preliminary question: What *is* a person and how far can the concept be stretched?

In a well-known analysis professor Strawson concluded to the primitive nature of the concept of person. The concept logically precedes that of a subject of states of consciousness as well as that of a subject of corporeal attributes, even though it requires both.[7] With regard to survival after death, Strawson concludes, as Morris Schlick and H. H. Price had done before him, that the state of a bodiless self can be made empirically intelligible only if we attribute to the person the same sensory components as in the present life with the exception of the bodily sensa.

> One has simply to think of oneself as having thoughts and memories as at present, visual and auditory experiences largely as at present, even perhaps—though this involves certain complications—some quasi-tactual and organic sensations as at present, whilst (a) having no perception of a body related to one's experience as one's own body is and (b) having no power of initiating changes in the physical condition of the world, such as one at present does with one's hands, shoulders, feet and vocal chords.[8]

Strawson is forced to concede that this would be a strictly solitary existence in which the individual is severed from all contact with, or even awareness of other individuals, and that the existence after death would be that of a *former* person forced to live exclusively on memories of the past. As they fade away, the awareness of the self must also recede. His description brings to mind the fate of the dead townspeople in Thornton Wilder's *Our Town*, who gradually lose interest in their past until they enter into total silence. Survival on those terms may well seem unattractive, Strawson admits, and the orthodox have done well to insist on the resurrection of the body.[9] Roland Pucetti rightly contends that the notion of seeing without eyes and hearing without ears is not sufficiently justified by the mere absence of logical contradiction.[10] That there may be little to say against the *logical* possibility of the hypothesis does not advance the argument a great deal and provokes Diderot's famous reply:

> If people can believe that they will see when they no longer have eyes, hear when they no longer have ears, think when they no longer have brains, love when they no longer have hearts, feel when they no longer have senses, or exist as objects when they have no extension and occupy no space, then they are quite free to do so, as far as I am concerned.[11]

Mr. Strawson may have thought of those objections himself, yet he provides us with no clue for answering them.

The Self and The Body

Could a more positive case be made for seeing without eyes and hearing without ears than the mere absence of logical impossibility? I know of only one serious attempt, made in an entirely different context, that could shed some new light on the problem. Joseph Maréchal in a remarkable analysis of mystical states has shown how the mystic may attain a vivid awareness of bodily presence unsupported by sense perception.[12] One cannot dismiss such feelings or the actual sense images by which they are occasionally accompanied, by calling them "hallucinations." For the existence of such hallucinations is the very problem to be solved. Maréchal shows the relative independence of the feeling with respect to the presence of actual sensations. Indeed, during those experiences or during states of mental dissociation actual sensations may fail to evoke a feeling of presence, while the "hallucinatory'' do. No associationist theory can adequately account for those phenomena, since it leaves unexplained the initial transition from internal representations perceived solely as modifications of the subject, to the awareness of an *external* object. Complexity and intensity of sensations fail to account for the feeling of presence, even though they may assist us in distinguishing afterward certain perceptions as truly objective from others which only seemed to be objective during the experience. The feeling of presence, then, is a primary experience which may occur even in the absence of perceptions that are normally needed to produce it.[13] It may adopt the more intellectual form of a spiritual presence, or it may emerge in the form of an actual perception. The term hallucination is usually reserved for the latter case.[14]

A somewhat similar case could be made for the functioning of memory without the support of the body. Already Bergson argued in *Matière et Mémoire* that this functioning is not dependent upon any specific part of the brain and that the psychic state, like the hidden part of an iceberg, extends farther than the cerebral state.[15] We might widen this discussion to include the entire relation of mind and body: consciousness can never be more than what William James termed a transmissive function of the brain. "In the production of consciousness by the brain, the terms are heterogeneous natures altogether; and as far as our understanding goes, it is as great a miracle as if we said, thought is 'spontaneously generated' or 'created out of nothing'." [16]

But if we grant—as every nonmaterialist would willingly do—that none of the mind's operations can be reduced to the body, what have we proven? That psychic acts transcend the bodily changes which support them. Yet do they prove that states of consciousness can dispense with the body *altogether?* I think not. For even the mystic remains bodily oriented. His body alone provides the stable vantage point which directs his experiences even when they transcend its ordinary capacity. Without any connection with a body the human mind would become totally disoriented. Even if memory were to be retained, and if a variety of perspectives simultaneously adopted were possible, such a radically new situation would seem to exclude any real continuity with the past.

The body is much more than an instrument of the mind: through it I define my relation to myself and to the world. Spinoza first in modern philosophy asserted the indissoluble union of body and mind. The mind to him is the idea *of the body*. Apart from the total elimination of the duality in materialistic systems—an *ignoratio elenchi* which we shall not consider here—the intimate connection of the two has been reasserted in the recent psychological theories of Klages and Merleau-Ponty. Klages echoes Spinoza: "The soul is the meaning of the body and the body is the manifestation of the soul; neither of the two acts on the other because neither of the two belongs to the world of things." [17] To be sure, the body may fail to express the mind: it may become a mere mechanism unable to convey meaning. A certain duality therefore appears to be inseparable. But nothing suggests that the mind would ever be able to dispense with the body as it is in the classical dualist positions of Plato and Descartes. All experience rather points to an operative union of mind and body so intimate that even the term causality cannot do justice to it. This becomes particularly obvious in linguistic expression. Clearly language is more than merely the body's vehicle for meaning. Meaning and language are constituted simultaneously.

Even the assumption of a "spiritual" body or a "new" body does not guarantee the survival of consciousness. For the intimate union of mind and body suggests precisely that personal identity is connected to a *particular* mind-body relation. A different body would jeopardize this identity. "It is essential to me not only to have a body, but to have *this* body." [18] Traditional theories of immortality mostly regard the body as an object in the world through which the mind acquires information that may be acquired in other ways. But the body is not a part of the world: it is my viewpoint with respect to the world.

> When I say that my foot hurts I do not simply mean that it is a cause of pain in the same way as the nail which is cutting into it, differing only in being nearer to me; I do not mean that it is the last of the objects in the external world, after which a more intimate kind of pain should begin, an unlocalized awareness of pain in itself, related to the foot only by some causal connection and within the closed system of experience. I mean that the pain reveals itself as localized, that it is constitutive of the pain-infested space. [19]

Theories of the mind-body relation such as the one from which this quotation was taken make it hard to conceive how any personal identity could be maintained apart from my present body. The Schoolmen therefore held that the mind's essential relation to a bodily existence persists in its separate state after death, and, indeed, that the soul remains incomplete until it is reunited with the body. Yet it still must be proven that a bodily oriented mind without a body (if I assume that concept to be a viable one) can preserve the continuity with a fully embodied existence. Most of the theories of immortality considered thus far dealt, in fact, with bodily oriented minds. In some (e.g., H. H. Price's theory) it is even difficult to decide whether the discussion concerns the survival of a bodily oriented mind or a reembodiment in a spiritualized body. Let us consider the case of reembodiment first.

Prior to the question whether a replica of the present body may be considered identical with the present body, we ought to investigate under what conditions reembodiment itself is possible. Clearly here also difficulties abound. No body is ever an isolated atom or monad. It is part of a relational whole situated in space and time, in which it communicates with other bodies. How could a new body possibly be related to the present universe? Does the universe of risen or spiritualized bodies occupy a space of its own allowing its bodies to communicate with one another but not with the ones in the present world? [20] This brings up the difficult question whether two different spaces could possibly coexist. Kant excluded this possibility in his theory that the various "spaces" (whose existence he problematically accepts) must ultimately be reduced to the one space form in accordance with which the subject arranges its sense data. This position allows for only one world of physical nature. Nor is it sufficient to conceive of simultaneously existing spaces as long as they remain totally unrelated to one another. Thus Leibniz's theory, according to which spaces are as numerous as the monads which they relate, advances our problem but little, and so do the non-Euclidean geometries of our own time. A theory of reembodiment requires that different spaces be *related* without being reduced to one another. A simple juxtaposition of the world of the living and the world of the dead as we find in the ancient myths and in the medieval Christian imagination would obviously not meet this requirement. For two spaces with a common point, such as the "passage" to the underworld or to the islands of the dead, are inevitably reduced to one space. Even to define one space as lying "outside" another is to use a reductive metaphor, since the "outside" belongs to the same space as the inside. What is needed is a relatedness of independent spaces in one consciousness.

William E. Hocking believed he detected an instance of this in the relatedness of dreams to the waking consciousness, or of the aesthetic space within a painting to that of the room in which it hangs. Although no interval exists between any single point of one space and a point in the other, the mind nevertheless easily passes from one to the other. The making of free decisions requires always a transition from existing space to possible space.[21] Fascinating as this solution is, it leaves a number of questions unanswered. One obvious question: How could there ever be a communication between the world of the dead and that of the living? H. H. Price readily conceded that the dreamlike world of mental images in which the dead move as in a Virgilian underworld contains no spatial relations with the land of the living. It would be a private world of individual mental processes.[22]

My problem with such a concept of unrelated bodies in an independent space is that it seriously weakens the meaning of the term "body." Are we still speaking meaningfully when claiming that after the destruction of his terrestrial body the individual continues to express himself through a "miasmic, subtle body"?[23] More seriously yet, can we consider the new body, whether it be a risen (i.e., recreated) or a diminished (e.g., a miasmic remainder) body, identical with the previous one? One ingenious attempt to cope with this difficulty consists in detaching the concept of survival from that of bodily identity. Thus Derek Parfit maintains that the person into whom a hemisphere of the brain of another person had been transplanted, could claim personal identity with the donor, provided he shared his memories.[24] Terence Penelhum has rightly and strongly argued against such a loose, psychological concept of personal identity which leaves it to the individual to decide what is his and what is not.[25] In view of the radical change entailed by death a carefully defined notion of personal identity is required. This requirement is obviously not met by the existence of some common elements in the *ante mortem* and the *post mortem* person.

The problem, however, with a discussion of this nature is that though all empirical criteria are lacking for establishing how much change is still compatible with actual identity, nevertheless, we are required to operate within restrictive parameters. In that sense the problem of survival is what Ninian Smart called an empirical question. It is not a priori impossible to *conceive* of the person in such a way that bodily death does not mark the end of the individual, but whether personal continuity can be preserved in any other way than through permanence in the same physical body cannot be a priori established.[26]

Beyond the Empirical Self

I consider it the prime merit of the empiricist position to have drawn attention to the basic deficiency of every a priori argument for immortality. Since no adequate empirical evidence is available of actual survival after death (I do not regard as adequate reports which we are unable to authenticate by rigidly scientific standards), we are forced to conclude that no conclusive argument for immortality can be given. Yet the weakness of the empiricist tradition consists in its inability to establish an adequate idea of the self. In the present discussion this weakness is manifest in the forever shifting ground of personal identity. Those who perceive the weakness of bodily continuity as basis refer to continuity of memory (Parfit's position). Those who see the inadequacy of such a subjective criterion (aside from the objections against Parfit's position, one need only think of the difficulty presented by the permanent amnesiac) return to the more objective ground of bodily identity. The fundamental problem of the empiricist position in this matter is that it is forced to rule also on the *possibility* of continuity on the sole basis of phenomena in which a change as substantial as death never occurs. Obviously no present experience could prove that the self *does* survive after death. Even the question whether it *could* survive cannot be decided without a notion of the self that exceeds the actual boundaries of experience.

Our criticism of the empiricist notion of the self must not be interpreted as an attempt to reintroduce a purely a priori concept of the self, pretailored to be immortal after the fashion of the ancient soul. Any concept of the self must be *supported* by actual experiences, even though the self may be more than the sum total of those experiences. Moreover, even if we are successful in expanding the notion of the self beyond a mere connection of conscious phenomena, the survival of such a self after death must in the end remain an empirical, and therefore unpredictable fact. At most we may be able to establish the positive possibility (i.e., more than the mere absence of contradiction) of life after death.

We are wont to identify the self with self-consciousness. But a moment of reflection shows that this identification cannot be consistently maintained. Although the self passes through prolonged periods in which it loses all awareness, no one could conclude therefrom that it has been suspended altogether. At all times philosophers have accepted the existence of a "dark side" of consciousness. With Leibniz this insight developed into a distinction between fully conscious apperceptions and half-conscious or subconscious *petites perceptions.* Yet the thesis of a relatively independent layer of unconscious selfhood gained more or less universal acceptance only through depth psychology. Of course, mystics of East and West had always known that the self is capable of overcoming the restrictions of ordinary consciousness. Mindful of their experiences W. Ernest Hocking sought to find a way out of the empiricist stalemate by positing a reflective self beyond the excursive, object-oriented one. This subphenomenal foundation explains how the self can remain constant after interruptions of consciousness and lapses of memory. The reflective self alone enables consciousness to recognize itself after having been separated from itself by a phase of unconsciousness.

> Why is this self, upon waking, the *same self?* Is it indeed because of the faithfulness of the physical world it deals with? Is it because this body and these walls are the same body and the same walls as yesterday? But the body and the walls of yesterday are gone: the body is indeed the same, but it is wholly incapable of presenting the self with the knowledge of that fact—it can work in the moment, it cannot retain its own past. It is the self which recognizes its body as the same; the physical constancy would be meaningless were it not for the underlying constancy of memory.[27]

This reflective self alone secures personal identity throughout variety and discontinuity. Steadfastly it maintains itself through the blackouts of consciousness and connects the intermittent stretches of consciousness. The body may be an indispensable instrument in this constant identification process but it cannot provide its ultimate foundation, since the body itself needs to be recognized as identical from one stretch to another. The self, then, surpasses the sum total of psychic phenomena. Indeed, the phenomena themselves remain unintelligible unless we accept a subphenomenal source from which they spring and which gives them their coherence. The founding self depends considerably less upon its bodily environment than the phenomenal self. The former's activity continues uninterruptedly after a withdrawal from the physical world in sleep, in trance, in artistic creation, or even in daydreams. Particularly in the latter two states we notice a strange interference of the unconscious with the conscious self. At such occasions, the self appears to be led beyond the boundaries of its ordinary world and to escape its ruling laws. It becomes expressive rather than reactive, revealing the workings of an inner power instead of those of its bodily world.

The deeper self depends less directly on its bodily situation than the ordinary self. In those mystical states in which it becomes predominant, sense perceptions cease to exist and purely mental visions take their place. Naturally, then, the question arises whether the self could ever dispense with its world altogether. Let me be clear that, though I regard no philosophical answer to this question conclusive, an unqualified affirmative seems to be excluded. Even if we grant it a relative independence, the mind seems to be so essentially and definitively determined by the body that it must forever maintain an essential relation to the body, if it is to preserve its identity. Whether it can do without full embodiment can philosophically be no more than a hypothesis. However, the "relative" embodiment of a self that is not dependent upon the actual presence of a body at least avoids such absurdities as "hearing without ears and seeing without eyes." Nor would the mind have to rely on past memories. If such memories persist at all, they are bound to become increasingly less significant and may eventually fade away altogether. The relatively embodied self must, rather, be seen as more expressive than it was in its previous state and stimulated primarily from within its own unconscious core. Whether we can move beyond this hypothesis and accept new external stimuli (as seems to be proposed in the doctrine of resurrection) entirely surpasses the scope of a philosophical investigation. Even a theory of relative embodiment can attain no higher philosophical status than that of a positive possibility.

One basic question remains. Can personal individuality be maintained throughout the substantial change of death? The question is closely connected with the one considered before: Can the identity of the person be preserved without permanence of the selfsame physical body? This, we concluded, was an empirical, although presently unanswerable question. Yet the preceding discussion allows us at least to define two conditions which must be satisfied for individual survival to be possible. (1) To survive individually the mind must maintain a permanent relation to an individual body. The body itself need not be permanent, but the mind must permanently retain the essential bodily orientation which makes it what Spinoza calls "the idea which expresses the essence of this or that human body under the form of eternity" (*Ethics* V, 21). Bodiliness of some sort, then, appears to be an essential condition for preserving personal individuality after death. (2) Under certain conditions the mind functions without depending on the actual presence of the body. Our earlier discussion of the feeling of presence concluded to the existence of individual states of consciousness in which the ordinary contribution of sense perception is suspended. It would be unwarranted to conclude therefore that the mind can ever function in total independence of a body. All we can claim is that at least *some* functions are both individualized and not *directly* dependent upon the actual presence of the body beyond the general physiological conditions (brain, nervous system, blood supply) of all conscious activity in the present life. This relative independence opens at least the possibility of states of consciousness that would require no actually present body. Yet, to be in accordance with the previous principle, even those states require some connection with an actual body although not necessarily a present one.

The preceding investigation leaves a number of basic questions unanswered. Can the mind after death maintain a sufficient continuity with its past existence to allow us to say that the same person survives? Can personal individuality be preserved in a state of relative disembodiment? All we possess beyond the mere absence of evidence to the contrary is one indication: certain phenomena show that the mind is not in all its functions directly dependent upon the contributions from the senses. This conclusion, however modest, still requires a notion of selfhood expanded beyond its ordinary empirical restrictions. But such an expansion is fully warranted by the findings of depth psychology and the experiences of mystics. Without taking full account of them, the very conditions for meaningfully asking the question of immortality are lacking. Yet once we widen the perspective so as to include the less common and, for most of us, indirect experiences of transcendence the question reemerges and takes on a new meaning.

8

The Mystical Experience of the Self

*Soul is a being that can be beheld by God and by which,
again, God can be beheld.*

HADEWYCH

The inward turn of religious recollection and the widespread belief in immortality or resurrection show the effective presence of a concept of selfhood which fundamentally differs from the one prevailing in common states of awareness. In the present chapter we shall attempt to focus on that concept somewhat more directly through the experience of the only persons who appear to have immediate access to its content—the mystics. Those who aim at the most intensive experience of the self have at all times believed that they would attain in the end a self no longer circumscribed by the bounds of ordinary consciousness. The very purpose of the mystical journey is to move beyond this consciousness into the dark source of selfhood. From their descriptions it would appear that many reach their destination. To them we must turn for knowledge nowhere else available.

The Religious Nature of the Soul

If we may attach any credence to the revelations of the mystics—and the universal nature of their experience forces us at least to consider their claims seriously—an altogether different layer of selfhood hides underneath the familiar succession of outward-oriented phenomena. Behind the gates to this restricted area the laws ruling ordinary consciousness seem to be suspended. Space and time recede or are transformed from a priori forms of outward perception into vistas of an inner realm with unknown rhythms and successions. From archaic depths the imagination (if it has not taken leave altogether) conjures well-structured visions known to the dream consciousness only through fragments and to the waking consciousness not at all. In privileged instances the intellectual intuition, so peremptorily exorcised by Kant's critique, reasserts its rights and the mind literally *perceives* as directly as the senses ordinarily do. The intellectual visions described by John of the Cross and Ignatius of Loyola are truly *visions* in that they belong to the order of perception even though all sensory input and perhaps all images have been halted. Does all this not support William James's observations that the ordinary, rational consciousness is only one kind of consciousness while all around it, separated from it by the flimsiest screens, there are potential forms of consciousness of a completely different nature? To James, the psychologist, a full knowledge of the self requires the contribution of the peak religious experience.[1]

The exceptional character of the mystical experience tempts us to isolate it from all others. But if its vision is unique, its foundation is not. For the mystical experience merely brings to full awareness the common religious principle that the soul itself rests on a divine basis. To the religious mind the soul is always more than it is: it transcends itself, so that the way inward must eventually become the way upward or downward (depending on the schema one adopts). This transcendence becomes manifest in the mind's self-understanding when the ordinary consciousness starts loosening its grip. At this point, religious man claims, we enter the sanctuary where God and the soul touch. It is also the very core of the self, as Eckhart so daringly expressed:

> There is something in the soul so closely akin to God that it is already one with Him and need never be united to Him. . . . . If one were wholly this, he would be both uncreated and unlike any creature.[2]

To lose one's God, then, is to lose one's deepest self, to become "unfree" and to be reduced to a "substance," a part of the world. Only in its capacity to transcend itself lies the soul's power to surpass the world altogether. The religious mind will find it symptomatic that even a creative theory of man, such as Marx's was, runs into difficulties with a concept of freedom that lacks true transcendence.

The concept of soul is originally a religious one. According to E. B. Tylor's theory, religion originates with the awareness of a ghost-soul that is able to wander away while the body remains stationary, and that eventually will leave the body altogether. Although Tylor's simplistically evolutionist and intellectualist interpretations of the primitive mind were later rejected, on one crucial issue he was undoubtedly right: the idea of soul itself emerges as a religious notion and remains so long after it has ceased to be primitive. Plato's view that the soul longs to rejoin the divine forms to which it is related sinks its roots into primary beliefs that long preceded philosophical reflection. To most North American Indians the soul was created separately by a god. Aake Hultkranz, the Swedish student of native American religions, does not hesitate to generalize:

> As a rule, the Indians of North America believe that man's spirit has its ultimate origin in the deity himself, either through creation or partial emanation. . . . A soul that is commonly considered to derive from the gods is *ipso facto* not an ordinary profane creation. Whether it is conceived to be a gift of the deity or an emanation of his being, it belongs through its origin to the supernatural world. The supernatural origin of the human soul finds particularly clear expression in the idea of pre-existence.[3]

We find similar concepts among Australian natives. To the Murngin tribe the soul is what lifts man above the profane existence and allows him to participate in the sacred values of an eternal civilization.[4] In the Greek mystery cult the soul is above all a subject of ecstasy, first in this life and eventually in the after-life.[5] According to Rohde the awareness of this ecstatic quality is what led to the belief in immortality.[6] The notion of a substantial soul itself may have been born out of the ecstatic experience and the concomitant belief in immortality.[7] In any event, it is certain that the archaic notion of the soul is mainly characterized by what Rudolf Otto calls "the element of feeling—stupor—which it liberates, and the character of 'mystery' and 'wholly otherness' which surrounds it."[8]

Even developed religious cultures have preserved this numinous quality. Thus much in the Upanishadic movement may be regarded as an attempt to penetrate that point of the soul where Atman is Brahman. The absolute is what I am in my true self: *Tat tvam asi*. The *Bhagavad Gita* describes the Atman in terms of the sacred: "marvelous," [9] "indestructible," "immutable," "incomprehensible." [10]

Christian theology regards the soul as created and is therefore more reserved, at least in its orthodox expression. Yet by no means did it "desacralize" psychology. The concept of the soul as an image of God determines the development of Christian mysticism as much as the notion of the Atman determines the Vedantic vision. The divine "character" of the redeemed soul, clearly present in St. Paul, was developed into a Christian psychology by the Cappadocians in the East and by St. Augustine in the West. The religious origin of their theories makes us all too easily overlook their psychological significance. To Gregory of Nyssa and Augustine the fundamental structure of the soul can be understood only from a transcendent perspective. Thus the first theologies of the soul were also the first attempts at depth psychology. Nor should we dismiss them as purely theoretical speculations. Whatever the quality of their interpretations may be, they were primarily attempts to articulate and to justify an *experience*.

The "Deeper Self" of the Mystics

I shall abstain from attributing more than a "characteristic" or typological significance to each particular mystical description of the self. Nor do I expect my elementary remarks in any way to disclose the phenomenological *essence* of the experiences. At this initial stage of what Whitehead called the "descriptive generalization," I feel unable to do more than to point at some striking differences between the ordinary self and the mystical self.

In fact the very existence of an essential difference presents the most salient point in mystical literature on the soul. Thus Ruusbroec clearly distinguishes the mystical awareness from the ordinary one: in the former, reason is suspended and the mind is emptied of all objects.

> Here our reason must be put aside, like every distinct work; for our powers become simple in love, they are silent and bowed down in the presence of the Father. This revelation of the Father, in fact, *raises the soul above reason, to an imageless nakedness*. The soul there is simple, pure

and spotless, empty of all things, and it is in this state of absolute emptiness that the Father shows his divine brightness. To this brightness neither reason nor sense nor remark nor distinction may serve; *all that must remain below;* for the measureless brightness blinds the eyes of the reason and compels them to yield to the incomprehensible light.[11]

A difference between two levels is universally suggested by metaphors of isolation, secrecy, height, and, of course, depth. St. Teresa speaks of the inner castle, Catherine of Siena of the interior home of the heart, Eckhart of the little castle, Tauler of the ground of the soul, the author of *The Cloud of Unknowing* of the closed house, Plotinus of the innermost sanctuary in which there are no images.[12] St. John of the Cross combines several metaphors in the second stanza of his famous poem:

> In darkness and secure
> By the secret ladder, disguised—oh happy chance—
> In darkness and in concealment
> My house being now at rest.[13]

Omnipresent are the images of depth.[14] Almost equally common is the image of height. The soul must "ascend" beyond images and understanding. In Plotinus this metaphor dominates, and the term "beyond" is the most significant one in the *Mystical Theology* of Pseudo-Dionysius, his Christian interpreter.

What characterizes the new state of consciousness above all is its qualitative distinctness. Ordinary psychic activity ceases to function, and the mind is "taken" into the ground of itself to which it has no independent access. In the *Katha Upanishad* we read:

> Atman is not to be obtained by instruction,
> Nor by intellect, nor by much learning.
> He is to be obtained only by the one whom he chooses;
> To such a one Atman reveals his own essence.[15]

Even the most cautious interpreters speak of "passive" states and "infused" contemplation. In the so-called quietist school passivity became the overriding characteristic of spiritual life.[16] In some texts of the Vedanta this mental passivity appears to exclude consciousness. Thus in the *Brhad-Aranyaka Upanishad* we read: "As a man, when in the embrace of a beloved wife, knows nothing within or without, so this person, when in the embrace of the intelligent soul, knows nothing within or without." [17] But no description ever surpassed the one found in the *Mandukya* of the fourth state of being, beyond dreamless sleep, in which all awareness of world and multiplicity totally vanishes.[18]

Those texts originated in a tradition which does not mince words when emphasizing the distinction between mystical and ordinary states of consciousness. Yet Christian writers, though more moderate in their expression, also strongly contrast the ways of discursive knowledge with the modes of contemplation. The entire Neo-Platonic tradition, which directly or indirectly includes most of Western mysticism, is expressed in Dionysius's paradox: "Into this Dark beyond all light, we pray to come and, unseeing and unknowing, to see and to know Him that is beyond seeing and beyond knowing precisely by not seeing, by not knowing." [19] John Tauler equally stresses the discontinuity with ordinary thought: "This inner ground of the soul is only known to very few people . . . it has nothing to do with thinking or reasoning." [20] St. Augustine's distinction between the discursive *ratio* and the *intellectus* which is directly illuminated by God's light [21] will be adopted by numerous spiritual writers after him. Richard of St. Victor describes the mystical ecstasy as a state of consciousness in which the soul is "cut off from itself." [22]

As reflection on the distinct states of consciousness increased, a theory of the activity of the "faculties" in the mystical consciousness emerged. In *The Dark Night of the Soul* St. John describes the transition from the ordinary to the spiritual level:

> In this state of contemplation which the soul enters when it forsakes meditation for the state of the proficient, it is God who is now working in the soul; *He bids its interior faculties* and allows it not to cling to the understanding, nor to have delight in the will, nor to reason with the memory.[23]

St. Teresa frequently refers to the paralyzation of the ordinary psychic functions, as in the following passage:

> When there is union of all the faculties the position is quite different. They can then do nothing, for the understanding is, as it were, dazed. The love of the will is stronger than the understanding, but the understanding does not know if the will loves, or what it is doing, in such a way as to be able to speak of it. As to the memory, my belief is that the soul has none, and cannot think at all; the senses too, in my opinion, are no longer awake, but are, as it were, lost, so that the soul may be more fully occupied in fruition.[24]

The preceding texts must not be understood as if all "faculties" ceased to function at once. We noticed St. Teresa's hesitation when she comes to memory. A nineteenth-century spiritual writer states explicitly: "The soul's powers are not always in the same degree of drowsiness. Sometimes the memory remains free, with the imagination." [25] Most of the time the "faculties" do not cease to function at all. They are "bound," which means that they no longer function in the ordinary way. The Spanish mystics insist that the will always continues to function, even though free choice no longer exists. But, above all, mystical states remain states of awareness, that is, cognitive states. Some mystics, especially in the Dominican school, consider ecstasy primarily an intellectual act, though not a discursive one. By several accounts also the imagination and the senses may become endowed with new powers. Thus the mystic in certain cases *sees* visions and *hears* voices, either with the senses or the imagination, which others do not perceive.[26] Are sensations which are not supported by ordinary sensory stimuli simply "illusions" as the term "hallucination" commonly implies, or can they refer to a different kind of reality? I consider a definite answer to this question impossible. But in any event the issue cannot be decided on the basis of the presence or absence of ordinary stimuli, as may be seen in Maréchal's essay "On the Feeling of Presence in Mystics and Non-Mystics." [27]

Yet a great deal of caution is required in interpreting references to mystical sensations. What John of the Cross describes as "touches" (*toque*) appears to be totally unrelated to those hallucinatory experiences in which the senses play a direct part and which remain therefore subject to errors of interpretation.

> When God himself visits it [the soul] . . . it is in total darkness and in concealment from the enemy that the soul receives these spritual favors of God. The reason for this is that, as his Majesty dwells substantially in the soul, where neither angel nor devil can attain to an understanding of that which comes to pass, they cannot know the intimate and secret communications which take place there between the soul and God. These communications, since the Lord Himself works them, are wholly divine and sovereign, for they are all substantial touches of Divine union between the soul and God.[28]

Repeatedly John insists that those touches occur "in the substance" of the soul, not in its faculties, and consequently, that they have neither form nor figure.[29] He seems to use the term "touches" to denote an experience unrelated to sensation but analogous to it by its directly intuitive character. The sense of touch was probably selected because of its greater immediacy and lesser distinctness.

As for the imagination, many spiritual writers attribute a new function to it in the visions and voices which usually precede the higher states of union. Imaginary visions may appear with the intensity of actual sensations, yet without any hallucinatory sensory experiences and often in fantastic or unprecedented forms.[30] It is as if images and symbols normally restricted to the unconscious are released when the mind first penetrates into the unknown depths of itself.[31] Jung has written memorable pages on this release of unconscious types and symbols.[32] The mystical vision structures this "unconscious" material according to its own intentionality. It would therefore be mistaken to place those visions on a par with ordinary dreams in which the same or similar material may appear. Indeed, St. Teresa points out that the imaginary vision is often accompained by an "intellectual" one which it renders more vivid and to which it gives a more lasting impact.[33] Nevertheless the upper levels of the unconscious appear to be more autonomous here than at any other stage of the mystical experience. Spiritual directors almost universally adopt a critical attitude toward this most sensational aspect of the mystical life. Zen masters as well as Christian directors caution the novice not to attach any importance to those apparitions.[34] Even if they come from God, St. John of the Cross warns us, they are "curtains and veils covering the spiritual thing." [35] True spiritual communication takes place on a deeper level, and all attention spent on those intermediate phenomena detracts from the direct contemplation of what remains beyond perception and imagination. Nevertheless St. John attempts to justify the existence of those imaginary visions and, in doing so, approaches a modern, psychological interpretation of the phenomenon.

> If God is to move the soul and to raise it up from the extreme depth of its lowliness to the extreme height of His loftiness, in Divine union with Him, He must do it with order and sweetness and according to the nature of the soul itself. Then, since the order whereby the soul acquires knowledge is through forms and images of created things, and the natural way wherein it acquires this knowledge and wisdom is through the senses, it follows that, if God is to raise up the soul to supreme knowledge, and to do so with sweetness, He must begin to work from the lowest and ex-

treme end of the senses of the soul, in order that He may gradually lead it, according to its own nature, to the other extreme of His spiritual wisdom, which belongs not to sense.[36]

A further discussion of those states belongs to the psychology of mysticism. Our present purpose is merely to explore what the mystical experience contributes to the knowledge of the self as such. From that point of view the highest states of mysticism, in which the so-called intellectual visions take place, are the most important ones, because they are totally unique and incomparable to any other experiences.

The Substance of the Soul

First it must be emphasized that there is more to those states than visions, even though we shall concentrate on them for practical reasons. Next, "intellectual visions" are not visions proper, since they do not consist of perceptions or images. Nor are they "intellectual" in the ordinary sense, since they are entirely nondiscursive and contribute nothing to the subject's "understanding" of himself and his world. Nevertheless, their main impact is one of insight and even of all-surpassing insight. Since the reader may not be familiar with descriptions of this kind of experience, I here relate two clear instances of it taken from Teresa and Ignatius of Loyola. Teresa writes:

> I once had such great light from the presence of the Three Persons which I bear in my soul that it was impossible for me to doubt that the true and living God was present, and I then came to understand things which I shall never be able to describe. One of these was how human flesh was taken by the Person of the Son and not by the other Persons. As I say, I shall never be able to explain any of this, for there are some things which take place in such secret depths of the soul that the understanding seems to comprehend them only like a person who, though sleeping or half asleep, believes he is understanding what is being told him.[37]

Even more typical is Ignatius's description of what he experienced at the river Cardoner:

> As he sat there, the eyes of his understanding began to open. Without having any vision he understood—knew—many matters both spiritual and pertaining to the Faith and the realm of letters and that with such clearness that they seemed utterly new to him. There is no possibility of setting out in detail everything he then understood. The most that he can

say is that he was given so great an enlightening of his mind that if one were to put together all the helps he has received from God and all the things he has ever learned, they would not be equal to what he received in that single illumination. He was left with his understanding so enlightened that he seemed to be another man with another mind than the one that was his before.[38]

The only mystic who has attempted to explain those experiences is John of the Cross. If I understand his interpretation correctly, the purely intellectual "apprehensions" may still have a certain sensory orientation in the sense that some affect the subject as visions would affect him, others as voices and still others as touches, yet always "without any kind of apprehension concerning form, images or figure of natural fancy or imagination." [39] If this is the case then Teresa's words make sense when she writes that "the Lord Himself in an *intellectual vision so clear that it seemed almost imaginary,* laid Himself in my arms." [40]

Still for our purpose it may be more profitable to concentrate on the purely spiritual content. All visions of this nature are short, ecstatic, and, in spite of their abundant spiritual light, somewhat obscure. Among the visions of incorporeal substances St. John of the Cross mentions a direct vision of the soul. He also claims that the intellectual experiences are "felt in the substance of the soul." [41] "God works then in the soul without making use of its own capacities." [42] From all evidence, we confront here unified states of consciousness which allow the soul to contact its own core. Let us subject this metaphorical language to a critical analysis.

First, even those unified states of consciousness retain a noetic quality which allows the mystics to refer to them as intellectual.[43] Yet the mind escapes the duality of ordinary consciousness. Taken literally, the expression "beyond dreamless sleep" in the *Mandukya Upanishad* would place the highest mystical state outside consciousness altogether. Yet the *Brhad-Aranyaka* explains: "Verily while he does not think, he is verily thinking." [44] However, the thought is not a second thing different from the thinker. This is indicated by John's claim that intellectual visions take place "in the substance of the soul" and by the various other expressions referring to substance at the end of *The Dark Night,* such as "His Majesty dwells substantially in the soul" and "substantial touches of Divine union between the soul and God." [45] Clearly the term *substance* alone appeared appropriate for that coincidence of being and knowing which precedes all mental differentiation.

Whatever else this knowledge may contain, it includes a unique and direct awareness of the self. Its direct character is all the more remarkable, since it is described entirely in negative terms. One attentive reader of the Christian mystics writes:

> The soul empties itself absolutely of every specific operation and of all multiplicity, and knows negatively by means of the void and the annihilation of every act and of every object of thought coming from outside—the soul knows negatively—but nakedly, without veils—that metaphysical marvel, that absolute, that perfection of every act and of every perfection, which is *to exist,* which is the soul's own substantial existence.[46]

Whether the right term is *existence,* as Maritain claims, or *essence,* as it is called by many mystics, all agree that we have here a direct, although negative, knowledge of ultimate selfhood, an immediate awareness of presence to oneself and to the transcendent source of the self. Such a direct intuition bypasses the channels of sensation and judgment by which the awareness of the self is usually attained. It neither needs nor provides any rational justification of itself. Confronted with statements such as "I felt that God was there: I saw Him neither with my bodily eyes nor through my imagination, nevertheless His presence was certain to me," [47] it is difficult not to accept the existence of a direct mental intuition in the mystical state. Most epistemologists have followed Kant in denying that the human mind ever attains such a *direct* insight into the presence of the real as such. Yet even Kantian students of the mystical experience are forced to admit that no other explanation remains.[48] For this fully conscious being-with-oneself cannot be accounted for by the categories of ordinary consciousness. The ordinary awareness of the self is achieved indirectly through a reflection upon its operations. Yet in mystical states we attain a direct, explicit awareness of the self *as such.*

> And this knowledge shows itself so radically different from ordinary knowledge, from the threefold standpoint of immediateness, mode and content, that the contemplative remains in the deepest stupefaction thereat. For in this case it is not amnesia which appears after the ecstasy any more than it was complete unconsciousness during it; the mystic remembers perfectly, but he does it through the belittling and dividing forms of the understanding which once more oppress him.[49]

Those words of Maréchal's echo John of the Cross' conclusion: "It is like one who sees something never seen before, whereof he has not even seen the like. . . . How much less, then, could he describe a thing that has not entered through the senses." [50]

In the Vedantic tradition the mystical knowledge of a self that remains hidden from ordinary awareness is all the more emphasized since the duality between man and Brahman is abolished. This fundamental self, unknowable yet attainable, is the ultimate reality. Shankara built his entire mystical philosophy on it. The "ground" of the soul, the Atman beyond all functions of consciousness, is the locus of mystical truth. This ground of selfhood is experienced by the mystics not only as hidden but also as transcendent. It is the very point in which the soul is more than an individual soul. Thus in the Vedantic tradition this deeper self is at once the core of all that is.

> The Inner Soul of all things, the One Controller,
> Who makes his one form manifold—
> The wise who perceive Him as standing in oneself,
> They, and no others, have eternal happiness. [51]
>
> Now, he who on all beings
> Looks as just in the Self,
> And on the Self as in all beings—
> He does not shrink away from Him. [52]

Text such as the preceding clearly indicate that the ground of the Self far surpasses the boundaries of individual personhood.

Christians tend to write this off as Oriental pantheism. But upon careful scrutiny they will find that their own mystics assert the transcendence of the mystical self. To them also at one point the soul and God are not two but one. We recall Eckhart's daring statement: "There is something in the soul so closely akin to God that it is already one with Him and need never be united to Him. . . . If one were wholly this, he would be both uncreated and unlike any creature." [53] Most Christian mystics have been less radical in their expression but not in their meaning. Thus Johann Tauler refers to the soul as a creature, but one standing between eternity and time, and with its supernatural part entirely in eternity. [54] Yet no one has elaborated the theme of self-transcendence more consistently and with more theological strength than Jan Ruusbroec. According to the Flemish mystic, man's true essence (*wesen*) is his super-essence (*overwesen*). Before its creation the soul is present in God as a pure image; this divine image remains its super-essence after its actual creation.[55] The mystical conversion, then, consists for Ruusbroec in regaining one's uncreated image. Through the mystical transformation (which Ruusbroec calls "overformation") the soul surpasses its createdness and participates actively in God's uncreated life.

> All those men who are raised up above their created being into a contemplative life are one with this divine brightness and are that brightness itself. And they see, feel and find, even by means of this Divine Light, that, as regards their uncreated nature, they are that same simple ground from which the brightness without limit shines forth in a godlike manner, and which according to the simplicity of the essence remains in everlasting, mode-less simplicity.[56]

To Ruusbroec the soul is from all eternity an archetype within God. To the extent that its actual existence in time is essentially connected with this archetypal image, it "dwells in God, flows forth from God, depends upon God and returns to God." [57] The nobleness which the mind possesses by its very nature, it cannot lose without ceasing to exist altogether. Now free, created mind may *actualize* the dynamic tendency of its nature "toward the Image" through a virtuous and God-seeking life. Yet a total identification can occur only through the passive graces of the "God-seeing" life. In the mystical state the mind comes to live "above nature" "in the essential unity of God's own being, at the summit of his spirit." [58]

Thus the ultimate message of the mystic about the nature of selfhood is that the self is *essentially* more than a mere self, that transcendence belongs to its nature as much as the act through which it is immanent to itself, and that a total failure on the mind's part to realize this transcendence reduces the self to *less* than itself. The general trend of our civilization during the last centuries has not been favorable to that message. Its tendency has been to reduce the self to its most immediate and lowest common experiences. But for this restriction we pay the price of an all-pervading feeling of unfulfilment and, indeed, of dehumanization. Deprived of its transcendent dimension selfhood lacks the very space it needs for full self-realization. With its scope thus limited freedom itself becomes jeopardized. Within such a restricted vision any possibility of meaning beyond the directly experienced is excluded.

Notes

Preface

1 Marx credits Hegel for this insight, but Hegel himself derived his dynamic concept of man from Fichte. Cf. *Economic and Philosophical Manuscripts*, in Karl Marx, *Early Writings*, trans. and ed. T. B. Bottomore (New York: McGraw-Hill, 1964), p. 202.

2 William F. Lynch, *Images of Hope* (Baltimore: Helicon, 1965), pp. 235–36.

Chapter 1

1 Edmund Husserl, *Die Krisis der europäischen Wissenschaften und die transzendentale Phänomenologie,* ed. Walter Biemel, *Husserliana: Edmund Husserl, Gesammelte Werke,* gen. ed. H. L. Van Breda (The Hague: Martinus Nijhof), vol. 6 (1954), part I; *The Crisis of European Sciences and Transcendental Phenomenology,* trans. David Carr (Evanston, Ill.: Northwestern University Press, 1970), part I.

2 Hans Blumenberg, *Die Legitimität der Neuzeit* (Frankfurt: Suhrkamp, 1966).

3 Thomas J. Altizer, *The Gospel of Christian Atheism* (Philadelphia: Westminster, 1966). Friedrich Gogarten, *Verhängnis und Hoffnung der Neuzeit* (Stuttgart: Friedrich Vorwerk, 1958); my own references are to the Siebenstern Taschenbuch edition of 1966. Carl Schmitt, *Politische Theologie: Vier Kapitel zur Lehre der Souveränität* (Munich and Leipzig: Duncker und Humblot, 1922). Hans Sedlmayr; *Verlust der Mitte* (Frankfurt: Ullstein,

1955). For an excellent survey of the entire problem, especially in its relation to Hegel, cf. Kenley Dove, "Hegel and the Secularization Hypothesis," in *The Legacy of Hegel,* ed. J. J. O'Malley et al. (The Hague: Martinus Nijhoff, 1973), pp. 144–55.

4   The objectivism of the modern age (especially scientism) is not "continuous" with late medieval religious thinking. In fact, it reacted strongly against it, especially against Scholasticism. But it was definitely prepared by it. It would be equally oversimplistic to attribute the rise of modern science to "objectivism." The success of science has encouraged the objectivist trend, but this is not essential to the scientific enterprise.

5   This, of course, does not exhaust the significance of Spinoza for the development of a theory of the subject, as we shall have occasion to mention.

6   Heidegger was to develop this principle at length in the third part of *Being and Time* which he never completed, but which is essential for understanding the scope of his work.

7   On this second alternative, cf. Friedrich Gogarten, *Verhängnis und Hoffnung der Neuzeit,* p. 173.

8   The term *Ideologiekritik* is applied to their work by Otto Pöggeler, *Hermeneutische Philosophie* (München: Nymphenburger Verlag, 1972), p. 36.

9   I have pointed out this lack of an ultimate *foundation* of Marx's critique of political economy in my work *The Philosophical Foundations of Marxism* (New York: Harcourt, Brace, 1966), pp. 213–30.

10   Max Scheler regards the drift toward pure objectivity in the West (present in its religion as well as in its science and technology) as the triumph of the practical Roman spirit over the more theoretical Greek-Oriental one. The hero and the saint (and today we may add the scientist) have replaced the sage (Max Scheler, *Die Wissensformen und die Gesellschaft* [Leipzig, 1926]). But I believe the origins to be older.

11   *Civilization and Its Discontents,* trans. James Strachey (New York: Norton, 1961), p. 33.

12   Ibid., p. 81.

13   *The Birth of Tragedy,* trans. Clifton Fadiman, in *The Philosophy of Nietzsche* (New York: Modern Library, 1954), p. 1046.

14   Ibid., p. 1029.

15   *Ecce Homo,* trans. Clifton Fadiman, in *The Philosophy of Nietzshe,* p. 936.

16   M. Heidegger, "Nietzsches Wort: Gott ist tot," in *Holzwege* (Frankfurt: V. Klostermann, 1950).

17   *The Portable Nietzsche,* ed. Walter Kaufmann (New York: Viking, 1954), pp. 137–38.

18   Gabriel Marcel strongly supported Nietzsche's conclusions on this point: "To the extent that God is identified with the super-sensible order in its entirety . . . it will become impossible for us, for example, to speak of the Good in absolute terms, for the Good will appear inseparable from an existential decision which is realized under certain determined conditions. . . . As soon as values allow themselves to be dissociated from this central affirmation, they break up, and at the same time each of them seems to lose its

vitality, to be reduced to its own skeleton, that is, in short, to something which one recognizes as a mere idea" (*Problematic Man*, trans. Brian Thompson [New York: Herder and Herder, 1967], pp. 37, 41).

19 Eugen Fink, *Nietzsches Philosophie* (Stuttgart: Kohlhammer, 1960), pp. 18, 15.

20 M. Heidegger, "Nietzsches Wort: Gott ist tot," in *Holzwege*, p. 238.

21 Marx considered the French materialism of the eighteenth century the direct outcome of Descartes's and Locke's theories on the one hand and of Bayle's religious scepticism on the other. Cf. *Die heilige Familie*, in *Marx-Engels Historisch-kritische Gesamtansgabe*, ed. D. Rjazanov (Frankfurt, 1972), I³, pp. 300–305.

22 Karl Mannheim, *Ideology and Utopia*, trans. Louis Wirth and Edward Shils (New York: Harcourt, Brace and World, n.d. [first edition 1936]), p. 17.

23 Alfred N. Whitehead, *Science and the Modern Mind* (New York: Macmillan, 1962), pp. 174–75.

Chapter 2

1 W. Robertson Smith, *Lectures on the Religion of the Semites* (1890; republished after the third edition by Ktav Publishing House, 1969), actually distinguishes the sacred from "the common," but it was this distinction which led Durkheim to the one between the sacred and the profane.

2 Emile Durkheim, *The Elementary Forms of the Religious Life*, trans. Joseph Ward Swain (New York: Free Press, 1965), p. 340.

3 According to Franz Steiner, *Taboo* (Baltimore: Penguin Books, 1956), pp. 87–88, taboo does not separate from the sacred but from the *common* which can still be sacred.

4 E. Evans-Pritchard, *Theories of Primitive Religion* (Oxford University Press, 1965), p. 65. The entire problem of the taboo as religious separation device was competently discussed in a recent publication by E. Zuesse, "Taboo and the Divine Order," *Journal of the American Academy of Religion* 42 (1974):482–504. His conclusion is unambiguous. "The deeper function of taboo, in short, is to define the divine life. It is *not* to keep man protected from entering into the sacred form from his 'profane' existence, but it is rather to keep man *in* the sacred order in all his existence" (p. 492).

5 In an article devoted to Eliade's theory of myth Jonathan Z. Smith questions the opposition sacred/profane in one particular instance. The chaos is not profane in the sense of neutral, as Eliade claims, but sacred in a negative way ("The Wobbling Pivot," *Journal of Religion* 52 [1974]:143). I suspect that the same principle would apply to every instance of "the profane" in a primitive culture.

6 The transcendence is reflected in the usage of the root q-d-sh. The verbal adjective *qadosh* is used for God (exclusively) and for persons (mainly), while the participle (mostly used as abstract substantive) *qodesh* is primarily applied to inanimate beings.

7 Exodus 31:13; Leviticus 20:8.

8   *Midrash Rabbah,* ed. H. Freedman, M. Simon, vol. *Exodus* (London: Soncino Press, 1939), p. 195.

9   Paul Mus, Avant-propos *Barabudur* (Hanoi, 1935), pp. 94–96.

10   H. Bouillard, "La catégorie du sacré dans la science des religions," in *Le sacré,* ed. Enrico Castelli (Paris: Aubier, 1974), p. 48.

11   J. Grandmaison, *Le monde et le sacré,* vol. 1 (Paris: Les Éditions Ourvrières, 1966), p. 26. Emphasis and translation mine.

12   Sociologists of religion also attribute an important part to cultural dissatisfaction in their interpretation of the religious attitudes today. But their argument usually adopts a less absolute form. It goes often as follows: Dissatisfaction with their present life forces our contemporaries to pose, once again, the *question of transcendence,* and leads many eventually back to some religious world view. Cf. Robert Nisbet, *The Social Bond* (New York: Knopf, 1970), esp. pp. 239ff.; Andrew Greely, *Unsecular Man* (New York: Schocken Books, 1972); and, most interestingly because most qualifiedly, Peter Berger, *A Rumor of Angels* (Garden City: Doubleday, 1967).

13   Robert Bellah, *Beyond Belief: Essays on Religion in a Post-Traditional World* (New York: Harper & Row, 1970), p. 227. For an incisive critique of the symbolic integration theory, cf. Charles Hardwick, "The Counter Culture as Religion," *Soundings* (Fall, 1973), pp. 287–311).

14   Thomas Luckman, *The Invisible Religion* (New York: Macmillan, 1967), p. 105.

15   Ibid., pp. 75, 85.

16   Antoine Vergote, "Equivoques et articulation du sacré," in *Le sacré,* pp. 490–91. My translation.

Chapter 3

1   Franz Rosenzweig followed the distinction to its brutal conclusion: "It is inconceivable, precisely from the side of individuality, that life should endure beyond the generation of progeny. And the endurance of individual life even beyond the years of procreativeness into old age is a completely incomprehensible phenomenon from a purely natural view of life" (*The Star of Redemption,* trans. William W. Hallo [Boston: Beacon Press,1972], p. 70).

2   Ibid., pp. 71–72.

3   As we shall see, Kant did accept a transcendent aspect in the ethical consciousness, very explicitly in the *Opus Posthumum,* and at least as a possibility in *Religion within the Limits of Reason Alone.* But in his ethical theory transcendence appears only in the extrinsic form of "postulates."

4   *On Religion,* trans. John Oman (New York: Harper, 1958), p. 37. This translation is based on the third edition of *Über die Religion: Reden an die Gebildeten unter ihren Verächtern* (Berlin, 1878).

5   *The Christian Faith,* trans. H. R. Mackintosh and J. S. Stewart (Edinburgh, 1928), p. 16. This translation is based upon *Der christliche Glaube, nach den Grundsätzen der Evangelischen Kirche* (Berlin, 1842).

6   *Dialektik* (Berlin, 1839). My translation.

7 *The Christian Faith*, p. 26.

8 *Either/Or* vol. 2, trans. Walter Lowrie (Princeton University Press, 1944), pp. 180–205.

9 Søren Kierkegaard, *The Sickness Unto Death* (Princeton University Press, 1954), pp. 168–69.

10 Franz Rosenzweig, *The Star of Redemption*, p. 73.

11 N. Kemp Smith, *A Commentary to Kant's Critique of Pure Reason*, 2nd edition, p. 638.

12 *Kants Opus Posthumum*, ed. by Erich Adickes (Berlin, 1920), p. 108. The transcendent foundation of the moral imperative may already have been implied in Kant's published writings on ethics. Referring to the latter, W. E. Hocking wrote: "Kant was dead-right in finding a sense of obligation at the center of our consciousness: there's an aboriginal I-ought which goes with I-exist.—The only point is, there is no obligation which is not an obligation to some living self, other than myself. The I-ought implies a Thou-art, coextensive with the world I am bound to think. That Thou is the self within the world, the one elemental Other. Its common name is God" (unpublished letter to Professor P. H. Epps of the University of North Carolina, written on October 14, 1954).

13 John Henry Newman, *A Grammar of Assent* (New York: Doubleday, 1958), p. 101.

14 Jacques Maritain, *Moral Philosophy* (New York: Scribner's, 1964), p. 79.

Chapter 4

1 William F. Lynch, *Images of Hope* (Baltimore: Helicon, 1966), p. 74.

2 *The Divided Self* (Baltimore: Penguin Books, 1965), pp. 51, 74.

3 Georg Simmel, "On the Concept and the Tragedy of Culture," in *The Conflict in Modern Culture,* trans. Peter Etzkorn (New York: Teachers College Press, 1968), p. 28.

4 William E. Hocking, *The Meaning of God in Human Experience* (1912) (New Haven: Yale University Press, 1962), p. 238.

5 Erik Erikson defines the negative identity as an attempt to regain some mastery over a situation in which the conditions for a positive identity are no longer available. Cf. "Identity and the Life Cycle," in *Psychological Issues,* vol. I, 1 (New York: International Universities Press, 1959): 131–32.

6 *Søren Kierkegaard's Papirer,* ed. P. A. Heiberg, V. Kuhr, and E. Torsting (Copenhagen, 1909–38), X², A 61. Alexander Dru, *The Journals* (New York, 1938), no. 970.

Chapter 5

1 Martin Heidegger, "What Are Poets For?" ["Wozu Dichter?" in *Holzwege*] in *Poetry, Language, Thought,* ed. and trans. Albert Hofstadter (New York: Harper & Row, 1971), pp. 94, 91. See also M. Heidegger, "Remembrance of the Poet" [in *Hölderlin und das Wesen der Dichtung*], trans.

Douglas Scott, in *Existence and Being*, ed. Werner Brock (Chicago: Henry Regnery, 1949), p. 284.

2   "The Origin of the Work of Art," ["Der Ursprung des Kunstwerkes," in *Holzwege*] in *Poetry, Language, Thought*, p. 72.

3   F. David Martin, *Art and the Religious Experience* (Lewisburg, Pa.: Bucknell University Press, 1972), p. 69.

4   In writing "appearance" I remain fully aware of a trend in painting, initiated by Cézanne, to represent objects not as they "appear" in the geometrical perspective of the Renaissance, but as they "are" in themselves. Thus a chair may show four legs, even though from his angle the viewer would be able to see only two, and a woman may display simultaneously a frontal and a side view of her face. Yet the significance of this innovation is that the artist concentrates on *appearing things* rather than on a particular spatial perspective within which they appear, not that he aims at the real as such.

5   G. W. F. Hegel, *Vorlesungen über die Ästhetik*, in *Jubiläumsausgabe*, vol. 12, p. 32. Comments in Karsten Harries, "Hegel on the Future of Art," *The Review of Metaphysics* 27 (1974): 677–699.

6   Ernst Bloch, *Das Prinzip Hoffnung* (Frankfurt: Suhrkamp. 1959), p. 248.

7   *The Other Dimension* (New York: Doubleday, 1972), p. 238.

8   Asia Society, *The Evolution of the Buddha Image*, selected by Benjamin Rowland (New York: The Asia Society, 1963).

9   Gerardus Van der Leeuw, *Sacred and Profane Beauty: The Holy in Art*, trans. David E. Green (New York: Holt, Rinehart and Winston, 1963), pp. 206–7.

10   *Das Prinzip Hoffnung*, p. 254.

11   See Walter Oakeshott, *The Mosaics of Rome* (Greenwich, Ct.: New York Graphic Society, 1967), p. 61.

12   The very word for God's glory, *kavod*, means effulgent light. To John "God is light" (1 Jn. 1:5) and Christ "the light coming into the world" (Jn. 1:9), while Paul addresses his Christians as "children of light and day."

13   André Grabar, *The Art of the Byzantine Empire* (New York: Greystone Press, 1967), p. 28.

14   Dietrich Seckel, *The Art of Buddhism* (New York: Greystone Press, 1968), pp. 186–87, 204–5.

15   Carlo Ossola, "Sospensione del tempo," in *Il simbolismo del tempo*, ed. Enrico Castelli (Padova: Cedam, 1973), pp. 35–57.

16   *Enchiridion Symbolorum*, ed. Denzinger-Bannwart (Barcelona: Herder, 1957), p. 337.

17   In depicting religious subjects Rembrandt frequently selected the moment of inner drama—Abraham answering Isaac's question about the sacrificial victim—rather than the outer event.

18   *The Meaning of Modern Art* (Evanston: Northwestern University Press, 1968), p. 154.

19   Cf. Jacques Claes, *De dingen en hun ruimte* (Antwerpen: De Nederlandsche Boekhandel, 1970), pp. 91–208.

20   Jacques Claes, op. cit., pp. 282–93.

21   Karsten Harries, op. cit., p. 107.

22   Søren Kierkegaard, *The Sickness Unto Death,* trans. Walter Lowrie (Princeton University Press, 1954).

23   Frank Kermode, *The Sense of an Ending: Studies in the Theory of Fiction* (New York: Oxford University Press, 1966).

24   The British critic Tony Tanner analyzes this desperate search for form in a universe that, through its own accelerating spiritual entropy, more and more disintegrates into pure structurelessness. "Words have to be organized in order to transmit any kind of information, and that organization is in itself a gesture against entropy. To counter entropy they must be organized in such a way as to defy probability; ideally this would mean using words in a way never before encountered. But here there is the danger of simply going beyond all organization, which in the long run is equal to the danger of submitting to probability. Either way the writer may find that the power of his words to transmit any kind of message or vivid information is perpetually in decline. Sometimes I think one can detect a sort of despair about language even in (perhaps particularly in) the most prolific American writers, a feeling about the inescapability of entropy such as is suggested by T. S. Eliot's line about working with 'shabby equipment always deteriorating' " (*City of Words* [New York: Harper & Row, 1971], p. 146).

25   David F. Martin, *Art and the Religious Experience,* p. 153.

26   Michael Seuphor, *The Spiritual Mission of Art* (New York: Galerie Chalette, 1960), p. 26.

27   Martin Heidegger, "What Are Poets For?" pp. 191–92.

Chapter 6

1   *Thus Spake Zarathustra,* trans. Walter Kaufmann, in *The Portable Nietzsche* (New York: Viking, 1954), p. 251.

2   Schelling, *Einleitung in die Philosophie der Mythologie,* in *Sämmtliche Werke,* vol. 2 (Stuttgart and Augsburg, 1856), p. 182.

3   Emile de Strycker, S. J., "Einige Betrachtungen über die griechische Philosophie in ihrem Verhaltnis zur antiken Kultur und zum modernen Denken," *Antike und Abendland* 20/1 (1974):8.

4   Rodolfo Mondolfo, *Problemi del Pensiero Antico* (Bologna: Nicola Zanichelli, 1935), p. 218.

5   T. S. Eliot, "Burnt Norton," in *The Complete Poems and Plays* (New York: Harcourt, Brace and World, 1952), p. 120. See also "Choruses from the Rock," ibid., p. 107.

6   Nicolas Berdyaev: "The interaction and clash between the eternal and temporal principles is that between life and death, for the final sundering of time from eternity, a victory of the temporal over the eternal, would signify the triumph of death over life just as the final transition from the temporal to the eternal would mean a severance from the historical process" (*The Meaning of History* [London: Geoffrey Bles, 1936], p. 68).

7   *Confessions,* trans. Frank Sheed (New York: Sheed and Ward, 1943), XI, 27.

8   Edmund Husserl, *Zur Phänomenologie des inneren Zeitbewusstseins* (1893–1917), ed. Rudolf Boehm, *Husserliana* (The Hague: Martinus Nijhoff), vol. 10 (1966), p. 202. I profited greatly from John Brough's beautiful essay "Husserl on Memory," *The Monist* 59 (1975), no. 1.

9   Ibid., p. 184.

10   Ibid., p. 292.

11   *Encyclopädie der Philosophischen Wissenschaften* (1830), nos. 451–52.

12   Our defective retention of the past was one of the main reasons which convinced the Buddha of the futility of the temporal process.

13   John Burbidge, "Concept and Time in Hegel," *Dialogue* p. 414. 12 (1973). This article shows well how the remembered past is always a diminished past. The author's argument on the relation between memory and a religious absolute, though presented from a different viewpoint, leads to conclusions similar to my own.

14   *Either/Or*, vol. 1, trans. David and Lilian Swenson (Princeton University Press, 1944), pp. 31–32.

15   Jean-Jacques Rousseau, *The Confessions*, trans. J. M. Cohen (Baltimore: Penguin, 1953), p. 114.

16   *Titan*, trans. Charles T. Brooks (Boston, 1864), p. 267 (the passage concludes the forty-fifth cycle).

17   According to Freud all poetic creation draws its phantasies from early and almost forgotten memories of fulfillment. Cf. his "Writers and Day-Dreaming," in *The Complete Psychological Works*, vol. 9, trans. James Strachey et al. (London: Hogarth, 1959), p. 147. An interesting illustration of the theory may be found in "Delusions and Dreams in Jensen's *Gradiva*" (*The Complete Psychological Works*, vol. 9, pp. 1–95) where a young archeologist dreams up an imaginary present out of his unconscious past, and then has to return to the historical past (the ruins of Pompeii) in order to discover his real present. Yet in the end Freud's most important contribution to aesthetic theory may well be one which he never recognized as such. By positing in *Beyond the Pleasure Principle* repetition itself as the most fundamental drive of the self, he provided us with a more adequate interpretation of the artistic impulse to recapture forgotten pleasures of the past.

18   Robert Penn Warren, "Rattlesnake Country," in *Or Else: Poems 1968–1973* (New York: Random House, 1974).

19   *Confessions* X, 25.

20   George Morel argues in *Problèmes actuels de religion* (Paris: Aubier, 1968), pp. 114–40, that the very experience of historical contingency is the awareness of an absolute ground. Cf. comments in Gerald McCool, "George Morel's Metaphysics of Historicity," in *Proceedings of the American Catholic Philosophical Association* 43 (1969): 101–108.

21   *Either/Or*, vol. 2, trans. Walter Lowrie (New York: Doubleday, 1959), p. 184.

22   *Being and Time*, trans. John Macquarrie and Edward Robinson (New York: Harper & Row, 1962), pp. 325–35.

23   Jacques Lacan, "Le stade du miroir," in *Ecrits* (Paris: Ed. du Seuil, 1966), vol. 1, p. 91.

24   Claude Lévi-Strauss, "The Effectiveness of Symbols," in *Structural Anthropology* (New York: Basic Books, 1963), pp. 186–205.

25   I. Hausherr, "Noms du Christ et voies d'oraison," in *Orientalia Christiana Analecta* 157 (1960): 160ff.

26   John Eudes Bamberger, "Mnēmē-Diathesis," in *Orientalia Christiana Periodica* 34 (1968), p. 246.

27   John Dunne, *A Search for God through Time and Memory* (New York: Macmillan, 1967), pp. 45–57.

28   Nicolas Berdyaev, *The Meaning of History,* p. 19.

29   Encyclopädie (1830) no. 565.

30   Franz Rosenweig, *The Star of Redemption,* trans. William Hallo (Boston: Beacon Press, 1964), p. 319.

31   T. S. Eliot, "Little Gidding," in *Four Quartets,* in *The Complete Poems and Plays,* p. 142.

32   Jean Wahl, "Time in Claudel," *International Philosophical Quarterly* 3 (1963): 493.

33   T. S. Eliot, "Burnt Norton," in *Four Quartets,* p. 121.

34   *The Mind's Road to God,* trans. George Boas (Indianapolis: Bobbs-Merrill, 1953), p. 23.

Chapter 7

1   Edward B. Tylor, *Primitive Culture* (1871). The quotation is taken from the second volume of a reprint, published under the title *Religion in Primitive Culture* (New York: Harper, 1958), p. 132. The interpretation of Marillier (*La survivance de l'âme et l'idée de justice chez les peuples non-civilisés*) and repeated by Remy de Gourmont (*Le chemin de velours*) and John Baillie (*And the Life Everlasting*) according to which immortality to the primitive is not a "religious" but a "scientific" conception is ill conceived. Since neither "science" nor "religion" exist independently to the primitive mind, the opposition between the two is meaningless. Yet if they mean that immortality is not a matter of specifically religious hopes but of a total view of life, their conclusion differs not too much from our own.

2.   John Baillie, *And the Life Everlasting* (New York: Oxford University Press, 1934), p. 204. It is clear, then, that we regard the unconscious refusal to accept the destruction of death an inadequate foundation for the religious belief in life after death. I do not deny the existence of a "primitive will to live," but I deem it insufficient to explain the faith in an afterlife of an entirely different nature. As representative of the unconscious desire theory, see Cavendish Moxon, "The Influence of Creative Desire Upon the Argument for Immortality," in *The Creative Imagination,* ed. Hendrik Ruitenbeek (Chicago: Quadrangle Books, 1965).

3   Alexandre Kojève, *Introduction to the Reading of Hegel* (New York: Basic Books, 1969), p. 251.

4   "Personal Survival and the Idea of 'Another World,' " *Proceedings of the Society for Psychical Research,* vol. 50, part 182 (1953), pp. 1–25; reprinted in John Hick, *Classical and Contemporary Readings in the Philosophy*

of Religion (New York: Prentice Hall, 1964), pp. 364–386. I shall refer to this reprint.

5   Op. cit., p. 369.

6   C. J. Ducasse, *Nature, Mind and Death* (La Salle, Open Court, 1951), p. 453.

7   P. F. Strawson, *Individuals* (New York: Doubleday, 1963), pp. 97–98.

8   Ibid., p. 112. On Schlick's position see Virgil C. Aldrich, "Messrs. Schlick and Ayer on Immortality," in *Readings in Philosophical Analysis,* ed. Herbert Feigl and Wilfrid Sellars (New York: Appleton-Century-Crofts, 1949), p. 172.

9   *Individuals,* p. 113.

10   Roland Pucetti, *Persons* (New York: Herder and Herder, 1969).

11   *Conversation with a Christian Lady,* in *Selected Writings,* ed. Lester G. Crocker, trans. Derek Coltman (New York: Macmillan, 1965), p. 262.

12   *Studies in the Psychology of the Mystics,* trans. Algar Thorold (New York: Magi Books, 1964), pp. 55-145.

13   Ibid., p. 102.

14   I must take sole responsibility for applying Maréchal's argument to the state of consciousness after death: Maréchal dealt exclusively with the mystical experience.

15   Henri Bergson, *Matter and Memory,* trans. Nancy Margaret Paul and W. Scott Palmer (London: Macmillan, 1911), p. xiii.

16   William James, *Human Immortality* (Boston: Houghton-Mifflin, 1898), p. 22.

17   *Vom Wesen des Bewusstseins* (Leipzig, 1921); cited in Maurice Merleau-Ponty, *The Structure of Behavior,* trans. Alden Fisher (Boston: Beacon Press, 1963).

18   Maurice Merleau-Ponty, *Phenomenology of Perception,* trans. Colin Smith (New York: Humanities, 1962), p. 431.

19   Ibid., p. 93.

20   Such appears to be John Hick's thesis when he posits the risen body as identical to the present one in all but its physical aspects. Roland Pucetti, who rejects Hick's thesis, points out that a total separation is the inevitable consequence of living in another time-space (*Persons,* p. 25).

21   William E. Hocking, *The Meaning of Immortality in Human Experience* (New York: Harper, 1957), p. 227.

22   H. H. Price, "Personal Survival and the Idea of 'Another World,' " *Proceedings of the Society of Psychical Research,* vol. 50, part 182, pp. 23–24.

23   Ninian Smart, *Philosophers and Religious Truth,* p. 188.

24   "Personal Identity," *The Philosophical Review* 80 (1971):3–27.

25   "The Importance of Self-Identity," *The Journal of Philosophy* 68 (1971):671.

26   In a famous dispute with M. Schlick, A. J. Ayer was challenged to show that his definition of the self as involving bodily sensation is the only one making sense within the reference frame of the English language. The fact that he could not do so proves nothing in favor of, or, against the possibility of

reembodiment. Cf. Virgil Aldrich, "Messrs. Schlick and Ayer on Immortality," in *Readings in Philosophical Analysis*, p. 173.
27 William E. Hocking, *The Meaning of Immortality in Human Experience*, p. 56. Wittgenstein also rejected memory as an adequate criterion for establishing the self's identity. Even if a person loses his memory he still continues to be the same person (*Blue and Brown Books* [Oxford University Press, 1969], p. 69). Nor did he consider the identity of the body or of conscious qualities a sufficient foundation. "The philosophical I is not the human being, not the human body or the human soul with the psychological properties, but the metaphysical subject, the boundary (not a part) of the world" (*Notebooks*, 1914–16, edited by G. von Wright and G. Anscombe [Oxford University Press, 1972], p. 82).

Chapter 8

1 Obviously I do not accept Erich Neumann's interpretation of the mystical types as corresponding to the three stages of life ("Mystical Man," in *The Mystic Vision*, ed. by J. Campbell [Princeton University Press, 1968], pp. 375–415). Such a reductionist projection is the exact opposite of what I have in mind. Instead of subsuming the unknown under the known, I want to expand the known by *adding* the novel *in its own right*.
2 *Meister Eckhart*, trans. Raymond Bernard Blakney (New York: Harper, 1957), p. 205.
3 *Conceptions of the Soul among North American Indians* (Stockholm, 1954), pp. 412–24.
4 W. Lloyd Warner, *A Black Civilization* (New York: Harper, 1964), p. 436.
5 Wilhelm Bousset, "Die Himmelsreise der Seele," *Archiv für Religionswissenschaft* 4 (1901): 253ff.
6 Erwin Rohde, *Psyche*, trans. W. B. Hillis (New York: Harper Torchbooks, 1966), pp. 264, 291.
7 Th. K. T. Preuss, *Tod und Unsterblichkeit in Glauben der Naturvölker* (1930), p. 17; cited in Gerardus Van der Leeuw, *Religion in Essence and Manifestation* (New York: Harper Torchbooks, 1963), p. 311.
8 Rudolf Otto, *The Idea of the Holy*, trans. John Harvey (New York: Oxford University Press, 1958), p. 194.
9 *The Bhagavad Gita*, trans. Eliot Deutsch (New York: Holt, Rinehart and Winston, 1968), 2, 29 (p. 49). R. C. Zaehner translates the term *ascaryam* (marvelous) as "*By a rare privilege* may someone behold it . . ." (New York: Oxford University Press, 1969), p. 50, while Rudolf Otto reads "*As wholly other* does one gaze upon it . . ." (*The Idea of the Holy*, p. 195).
10 Ibid. (Deutsch) 2, 17–18 (p. 38). A similar idea is expressed in the *Visnu-smrti* 20, 53.
11 *Spieghel der eeuwigher salicheit*, in *Werken*, vol. 3 (Tielt: Lannoo, 1947), p. 212.
12 *Enneads* VI, 9, 11.

13 *Dark Night of the Soul*, trans. E. Allison Peers (New York: Doubleday, 1959), p. 34.

14 William Johnston describes the mystical process in *The Cloud of Unknowing* as a descent to "the still point or the ground of the soul" in which "the mind goes silently down into its own center, revealing cavernous depths ordinarily latent and untouched by the flow of images and concepts that pass across the surface of the mind" (*The Still Point* [New York: Harper & Row, 1971], p. 132).

15 R. E. Hume, *Thirteen Principal Upanishads* (New York: Oxford University Press, 1931), *Katha* 2, 23 (p. 350).

16 One of the propositions endorsed by Molinos and condemned by Pope Innocent XI reads: "Doing nothing the soul annihilates itself and returns to the source and origin, the essence of God, in which it remains transformed and defined. God remains in Himself because then there are no longer two things united but one sole thing. In this way God lives and reigns in us and the soul annihilates itself in the very source of its operations" (Denziger-Bannwart, *Enchiridion Symbolorum*, no. 1225; trans. Elmer O'Brien, *Varieties of Mystic Experience* [New York: Holt, Rinehart, 1964], p. 304).

17 *Brhad-Aranyaka* 4, 3, 21; Hume, p. 136.

18 *Mandukya* 5; Hume, p. 392.

19 *Mystical Theology*, in Migne, *PG*, III, 1000; trans. Elmer O'Brien, *Varieties of Mystic Experience*, p. 83.

20 *Sign Posts to Perfection: A Selection from the Sermons of Johann Tauler*, ed. and trans. Elizabeth Strakosch (St. Louis: Herder, 1958), pp. 95–96.

21 In *Joan. Evang.* 15, 4, 19. On this distinction, cf. Etienne Gilson, *The Christian Philosophy of St. Augustine*, trans. L. E. M. Lynch (New York: Vantage Books, 1967), p. 270.

22 On the basis of the Vulgate translation of *Hebrews* 4, 12 he distinguishes *anima* and *spiritus*. Cf. *Selected Writings on Contemplation*, ed. and trans. Clare Kirchberger (London: Faber and Faber, 1957), p. 204.

23 *The Dark Night of the Soul* I, 9, 7; Peers trans., p. 67.

24 *Relations* V, in *The Collected Works of St. Teresa*, trans. E. Allison Peers (London, 1934–35), vol. 1, p. 328.

25 Picot de Clorivière, *Considérations sur l'exercice de la prière* (1802), quoted in A. Poulain, *The Graces of Interior Prayer* (St. Louis: Herder, 1910), p. 78. Why so much special attention is given to memory will appear further in this chapter.

26 Scaramelli in his renowned *Directorio mistico* (1754), treatise 3, no. 32, does not hesitate to use the term "sensation" for those direct perceptions. Luis de la Puente distinguishes separate senses: "As the body has its exterior senses, with which it perceives the visible and delectable things of this life, and makes experience of them, so the spirit with its faculties of understanding and will, has five interior acts corresponding to these senses, which we call seeing, hearing, smelling, tasting and touching spiritually, with which it perceives the invisible and delectable things of Almighty God, and makes experience of them" (*Meditations*, as quoted in Poulain, op. cit., p. 101).

27 In *Studies in the Psychology of the Mystics,* trans. Algar Thorold (Albany: Magi Books, 1964), pp. 55–146.

28 *Dark Night of the Soul* II, 23, 11. Cf. also II, 23, 5 and *The Living Flame of Love,* trans. E. Allison Peers (New York: Doubleday, 1962), stanza II, 16 (pp. 67–68).

29 *The Living Flame of Love,* st. II, 7 (p. 62).

30 Teresa describes the imaginary vision as being "so clear that it seems like reality" and "a living image" which the imagination is unable to produce in its ordinary functioning. "How could we picture Christ's Humanity by merely studying the subject or form any impression of His great beauty by means of the imagination?" (*The Autobiography of St. Teresa of Avila,* trans. and ed. E. Allison Peers [New York: Doubleday, 1960], pp. 268, 261, 262).

31 In writing "first" I do not wish to imply that those states are restricted to one particular stage of development. They may be part of a recurring experience, as they clearly were in St. Teresa's case.

32 *Psychology and Religion: West and East,* trans. R. F. C. Hull (London, 1958), pp. 542–52. Jung's interpretation was vaguely anticipated by William James, *The Varieties of Religious Experience* (New York: Collier Books, 1961), p. 375, and, uncritically, by H. Delacroix, *Etudes sur l'histoire et la psychologie des grands mystiques chrétiens* (Paris, 1908).

33 "Though the former type of vision [the intellectual], which, as I said, reveals God without presenting any image of Him, is of a higher kind, yet, if the memory of it is to last . . . it is a great thing that so divine a Presence should be presented to the imagination and should remain within it. These two kinds of vision almost invariably occur simultaneously" (*The Autobiography of St. Teresa of Avila,* p. 263).

34 William Johnston, explaining the suspicion with which the phenomena of the "makyo" stage in the developing Zen enlightenment are regarded, interprets it as the rising of the unconscious into the conscious mind (*The Still Point: Reflections on Zen and Christian Mysticism,* pp. 10, 50). St. John of the Cross claims that "both God and the devil can represent the same images and species" (*The Ascent of Mount Carmel,* trans. and ed. E. Allison Peers [New York: Doubleday, 1958], II, 16, 3). Even Teresa, who reports some of her most striking visions as having been of this kind, nevertheless adds that they are open to "illusions of the devil" and that she herself has been deceived by them (*Autobiography,* ch. 28, esp. pp. 259, 263).

35 *The Ascent of Mount Carmel* II, 16, 11; also, II, 19.

36 Ibid. II, 17, 3.

37 *Relations,* in *Works,* vol. 1, p. 362.

38 *Obras Completas de san Ignacio de Loyola* (Madrid, 1952), pp. 49–50; trans. Elmer O'Brien, *Varieties of Mystic Experience,* p. 247.

39 *The Ascent of Mount Carmel* II, 23, 3.

40 *Relations, Works,* vol. 1, p. 364.

41 *The Ascent of Mount Carmel* II, 24, 4, and II, 24, 2.

42 Ibid. II, 26, 5.

43 William James was undoubtedly right in ascribing this quality to all mystical states. Cf. *Varieties of Religious Experience,* p. 300.

44 *Brhad-Aranyaka* 4, 3, 28; Hume, p. 137. Teresa, in a text which strongly emphasizes the total passivity of the experience, qualifies her assertion about the lack of knowledge: "Here we are all asleep, and fast asleep to the things of the world, and to ourselves" (*Interior Castle* [Fifth Mansions], trans. E. Allison Peers [New York: Doubleday, 1961]), p. 97.

45 *Dark Night of the Soul* II, 23, 11.

46 Jacques Maritain, *Redeeming the Time* (London: Geoffrey Bles, 1946), p. 242. Maritain distinguishes between the "natural" mystical experience, in which the soul is attained directly and God indirectly, and the "supernatural" in which God is attained directly (p. 246). I am not sure that such a distinction can be consistently maintained on a theological level, much less on a philosophical. In all religious mysticism the self is immediately perceived *in* its transcendent dimension or, in Maritain's language, in its "sources."

47 Luis de la Puente, *Vida del P. Balthasar Alvarez* (Madrid, 1615), ch. XV; trans. and quoted in Poulain, *The Graces of Interior Prayer*, p. 83.

48 This is especially the case for Joseph Maréchal (cf. *op. cit.*, pp. 102, 196). But we find it also in Rudolf Otto, *Mysticism East and West*, trans. Bertha L. Bracey and Richenda C. Payne (New York: Macmillan, 1932 [1970]), pp. 50–88, and, with some qualifications, in the Thomist Jacques Maritain, *Distinguish to Unite*, trans. Gerald Phelan (New York: Scribner's, 1959), pp. 261 ff. and 446–50. Compare with St. Thomas, *Summa Theologiae*, II–II, 180, 5.

49 Joseph Maréchal, *op. cit.*, p. 192.

50 *Dark Night of the Soul* II, 17, 3.

51 *Katha Upanishad* 5, 12; Hume, p. 357.

52 *Isa Upanishad* 6; Hume, p. 363.

53 Sermon "Qui audit me, non confundetur," in *Meister Eckhart*, trans. Raymond Bernard Blakney (New York: Harper, 1957), p. 205.

54 "Sermon for Christmas," in *Signposts to Perfection*, selected and trans. by Elizabeth Strakosch (St. Louis: Herder, 1958), pp. 3–4.

55 *Spieghel der eeuwigher salicheit*, in *Werken*, vol. 3, p. 167.

56 *Die gheestelike brulocht*, in *Werken*, vol. 1, p. 246; *The Adornment of Spiritual Marriage*, trans. Wynschenck (New York: Dutton, 1916), p. 174.

57 *The Adornment of Spiritual Marriage*, p. 127.

58 Ibid., p. 130.